FROM COALPIT TO PULPIT

FROM COALPIT TO PULPIT

Fredrik W. Edwardy

Review and Herald Publishing Association
Washington, DC 20039-0555
Hagerstown, MD 21740

Copyright © 1983 by the
REVIEW AND HERALD PUBLISHING ASSOCIATION

Editor: Thomas A. Davis
Book Design: Robert Wright
Cover: Lou Skidmore

Library of Congress Cataloging in Publication Data
Edwardy, Fredrik W.
   From coalpit to pulpit.

   1. Shuler, John Lewis, 1887-   . 2. Seventh-day
Adventists—Clergy—Biography. 3. Clergy—United States—
Biography. I. Title.
BX6193.S58E38   286.7'3 [B]   81-23549
ISBN 0-8280-0110-3

Printed in U.S.A.

CONTENTS

PREFACE

There can be no limit to the usefulness of anyone, educated or uneducated, when he or she puts self aside, makes room for the leavening influence of the Holy Spirit within, and dedicates each day to the service of God. Such dedication shines through the life story of John Lewis Shuler from the time of his conversion. As a young man with only a ninth-grade education he threw down his shovel in a coalpit and took his Bible into the pulpit to proclaim God's good news. Undoubtedly, he became the most prominent leader in Seventh-day Adventist evangelism in America during the thirties and forties.

The Author.

1

PREMONITION

ohn Lewis Shuler! You standin' there talkin' to yourself in the mirror? Shame on you! I declare, boy, I don't know what's gonna become of you. Workin' in the mine don't bring out the man in you like it has your father!"

John's mother stood for what, to John, seemed a long moment, shaking her head dubiously, pausing in her censure long enough to pin back a stray lock that had tumbled across her forehead.

"Your father's through with the tub, so stir yourself, son," she said, her voice softening suddenly. "Hurry and get cleaned up. Supper's almost ready."

Mother Shuler turned abruptly to hide an unaccountable tear that blurred her vision. She hurried downstairs to stir the stew bubbling on the wood-burning stove.

Fifteen-year-old John had not turned to face her. He was blushing hotly. How much had she heard of his ranting to his image in the mirror? Good thing she couldn't see him blush, he thought. It was small comfort to know there was some advantage in being coated with a thick veneer of coal dust and sweat. Besides, blushing was nothing new to John; it was as commonplace as talking to himself, but only he was aware of that.

Given to much philosophizing during the hours he spent alone in the mine, John found the practice was not easy to break when he came home to the family. Unwittingly, standing in the shadows of late afternoon before his mirror with only the whites of his eyes visible, he had paraphrased Macbeth. In the mirror his eyes were like shapes cut out of a large piece of black paper. All else was lost in deep shadows. Somehow it seemed to suggest the futility of his life. Perhaps it was his mumbling about that which his mother had heard. One day was only a carbon copy of another, with John and his father returning from long hours spent in the fetid Farmington coal mine looking like two blackfaced comedians. Only there was nothing to laugh at.

Such a routine couldn't be much different from laboring with a chain gang or serving a term in a Siberian prison camp. For all he knew, the situations were the same—except here there was no guard with a gun. But still there was a similarity: he received no wages, his labors simply being added to the earnings of his father, who saw to it that John put in as many hours as he himself did.

Prodded back to the moment by his mother's impatient call echoing up from the kitchen, John stomped wearily downstairs and out to the back yard to take down the galvanized washtub from its peg on the porch where his father had just hung it. It was still warm, even after being emptied of its inky contents. John filled half the tub with cold water from the pump, took it inside the enclosed porch, and added a bucketful of steaming water from the reservoir heated by the kitchen stove.

In less than five long-practiced minutes he had tossed off his heavy mining togs, stepped into the tub, and poured a bucket of warm water over his head before soaping up and rinsing. Freshly laundered clothing had been laid out for him by his mother. He emerged, scrubbed to pale pinkness, with hair combed, ready to take his place at the table.

Being the eldest of three boys and three girls, John Lewis sat across from his father at the far end of the table. But it was not symbolic of his being second in command of the household. His father ruled with an iron hand. Being the son of a German immigrant, he had adopted his own father's imperialistic line of family command: you listened when he spoke, you jumped when he "cracked the whip." There was no whip, of course; just seeing the ripple of his bulging biceps, you did his bidding without question.

John never tired of telling his friends how on several occasions his father had jumped into the milewide Mississippi at Rock Island, Illinois, to swim the crosscurrent to Davenport, Iowa. It was easy for him. His powerful forearms were larger than John's thighs. John Lewis, unfortunately, had inherited the slender build of his mother, but he was a couple of inches taller than his father.

Tonight, as usual, the family ate in silence, only the crackling of the fire in the stove could be heard above the occasional clink of fork or knife on plate. There had been no grace said before the meal. There never was; the Shulers were a churchless family. Not that any of them were unmindful of there being a God; they were simply unpracticed in thinking about Him, and not one of the four or five churches in Farmington had ever bothered to invite them to attend services, much less to join their congregation, which fact suited the Shuler family just fine.

But this night turned out to be not exactly as usual. While John had been taking his bath, a neighbor had rapped on the front door and told Father Shuler about a cave-in at a mine in a neighboring town. Thirteen unfortunate men were still trapped, and there might be a call for miners to help dig them out. Several of the missing men were from families they knew.

Between mouthfuls and in monosyllables the head of the Shuler family informed the seven heads attentively turned toward him of what had happened and that he and John might be called for "volunteer" service.

John stayed home after supper so he would be available in case the call came. Usually he spent two or three nights a week with his friends, playing poker, drinking beer, and doing anything he could to compensate in a small way for the drabness of his workaday world. During the school term, his studies kept him occupied and diverted to some extent. Now that it was summer, there were only weekends and evenings that allowed time for whatever change of pace he and his friends could dream up.

He was looking forward to the coming Saturday and Sunday for a number of reasons. He and several of his buddies, three of whom were also miners' sons who worked in the mine, and, like himself, were out to kill dull routine in any way possible, were building a dam at the far end of a neighbor's farm, where they had found a suitable place for a swimming hole. In their characteristic youthful impulsiveness they had neither bothered to ask the owner's permission nor realized that blocking the small stream for any length of time might stop the farmer's irrigation schedule and jeopardize his crop.

Another of their ventures was not without a real hazard. They had taken a leaf from one of their school books that told about William Tell's shooting an apple off a boy's head. But they had gone Tell one better and were practicing shooting the *ashes* from one another's cigarettes at ten paces. However, even they were growing apprehensive as they gradually widened the distance between the rifle and their tiny target. Perhaps, if it had not been for the approaching turn of events in John Lewis' life, a tragedy might have ended one of their young lives, as is all too often the case with impetuous teen-agers seeking momentary thrills.

The night passed uneventfully, with no call for help from the mine with the cave-in. John and his father awakened at the regular hour, had their breakfast and started off with their lunch boxes packed by a silent, dutiful mother and wife.

It was nearly an hour before daybreak. As far as the rest of the inhabitants in the sleepy mining village were concerned, it was still the dead of night. The clatter of their stiff leather boots on the loose coal echoed in the vaulted mine tunnel entrance.

Following in the footsteps of his father, John entered the elevator cage and gave the customary yank on the rope that signaled the engineer to lower away. Above them, hidden in the darkness that bore down on them, was a slender one-inch cable supporting their cage—and their lives. It ran up and over a pulley at the top of a tower seventy feet above them and was connected to a huge steel drum in the engine room. Thinking of how his life hung on that cable, John decided that *faith* wasn't quite the right word to describe his attitude to it. Perhaps *reliance* was more fitting. Sometime he'd have to look up the difference in word meaning.

Except for the tiny oil lamps on their caps, the blackness could almost be felt. It was a relief to be met at the bottom of the shaft by eight of the other miners on this shift who had waited to walk with them for the more than a mile to the adjoining shafts where they would be working. With their combined lights, it made walking easier. Besides, they could share the latest news about the cave-in. Bud Rankin, a boy about John's age, paired off with him, and they fell in behind the others.

"Didja hear about the Thompsons?" Bud asked hoarsely.

"N-n-n-no," John stammered. "S-s-some of th-th-them g-g-get h-hurt?"

One of John's greatest handicaps was stammering. It was especially noticeable when he was under stress, and such seemed to be his case most of the time of late. No one else in the family was thus afflicted, and he endured much teasing from his brothers, sisters, and schoolmates. He'd tried every suggested remedy— even to holding pebbles on his tongue as the Greek orator Demosthenes did—but nothing helped.

"Ya, the three of his oldest boys an' old man Thompson, working the same shift, were smashed flat when the timbers gave way in their shaft after the blast. The others who were trapped were dug out unhurt last night."

Bud rattled on, but John's mind was abruptly immobilized as though mired in quick-setting cement. Not one word of Bud's additional comments made an impression on John's brain, though he made some laconical comments that apparently satisfied Bud. The nightmarish dread of sudden annihilation under tons of coal that had plagued him when he had begun work at 14 now returned with the silent, smothering sensation he imagined came with the fluttering wings of impending death. There had never been a disaster in this mine, but statistics were always ripe for such an event right here and now—this very shift perhaps.

This could well be another "tale told by an idiot," as he remembered Shakespeare had characterized life. It was for the Thompsons!

That day, as John used the pick and drill, he worked mechanically, hardly aware of what he was doing. The accumulation of his entangled emotions defied unraveling; the ignorance, the helplessness, the baffling purposelessness of daily, somnolent labor defied any reasoning for their existence. As he and his father walked back to the elevator cage at the end of their shift, he seemed to be trudging dutifully to some timeless, zombie cadence. He was mired in a black somberness, haunted by some unseen specter that told him it was imperative for him to escape before the same fate that had befallen the Thompsons overtook him also.

2

ANTICIPATION

As the days followed monotonously in each wearying week of work at the mine, John Lewis did not find monologuing an easy habit to break himself of. Nor did he think it strange that he seldom stuttered when talking to himself. Accepting these facts without question, he pitted one reason against another, seeking some rationale for what the future might hold for him.

"That's right, Old John," he scolded himself, "bear down on that drill with all your might—maybe someday your arms will bulge with muscles like your father's." There was nothing like setting your heart on a goal, even if you knew you'd never make it, he reasoned. But aloud he stated the fact: "You lie, and you know it! You've got the bones of a sparrow. There is nothing there to build muscles on," he growled, pinching the girth of his slender biceps that showed only the slightest bulge beneath his sweat shirt.

Doggedly gritting his teeth while putting all his weight against the hand-cranked coal drill, John turned the handle with all his might, stopping momentarily every few seconds to catch his breath. Sweat poured down his face, making tiny white rivulets in the black coal dust that powdered his skin. Between grunts and panting for breath, the drill was forced on and on, deep into the coal, until he had reached a depth of seven feet. Only then did he take a short breather while preparing the next step in the blasting routine.

"Roll the paper tight, John," his boyish voice echoed in the long tunnel, "you've got to keep the tube thin enough so it'll slide down the hole. There, you've got it! Now you're ready for the blasting powder."

For safety's sake he took off his cap, with its flickering oil lamp, and placed it to one side lest it ignite a premature blast while the powder was being handled. The sweat was now cold on his forehead because of a sense of apprehension. In fact, the possibility of an accident—especially during the blasting routine—subconsciously was never dimmed.

However, there was no thought of asking for divine aid or protection during these moments of peril. He had never been one to dwell on the thought that his life was of the slightest interest to God. Having always been irreligious, he scoffed good-naturedly at churchgoers among his friends, and their addiction to heeding the counsel of "sky pilots."

After filling the tube and fashioning a fuse several feet long, John sat back and mopped his brow.

"If I thought I'd be doing this for the next forty years, I'd probably shoot myself right now," he muttered matter-of-factly, running his tongue over his blackened lips.

Besides being arduous employment that gave it every reason to be dreaded, coal mining also had insidious, invisible hazards you could never actually touch or get a grip on. In battling them it didn't matter that you had the herculean strength of a man like his father. Among these dreads was the constant possibility of running into carbon dioxide, a nonexplosive gas, that suffocated all who breathed it for long. It was called chokedamp. Then there was methane, which the miners called firedamp. Firedamp, when mixed with air, quickly became explosive, so any time its presence was suspected, a miner put out his lamp and dared not relight it until he was certain that the pit had been sufficiently ventilated.

Although he had been well drilled regarding the dangers in the mine when he had first come into the pits to work beside his father a year ago, he had never become numbed to the job's numerous threats to life and limb.

One point on which he was positively clear: he would never be content to follow in his father's footsteps, much as he admired him physically. And there was much to be admired in the man. Not only was he a hard worker who was capable of earning a better living than the average miner and who had supervisory duties, but he was also a skilled carpenter, having himself built a large frame home for his family. As each child had been born he had added another room, until he had been forced to raise the roof. The house had now become a two-story, ten-room country home, and John had been given a large room on the second floor at the head of the stairs.

He had been reluctant to move from his ground-floor room next to the kitchen. Not that he disliked his new quarters, but living on the second floor put an end to his using the escape route he had from his old room. When his mother had women friends in to visit in the parlor, John was too bashful to be seen slipping out through the kitchen or making it to the front door without speaking or being spoken to. Escaping without being put through this torturous obligation was simply a matter of sliding out the window and dropping three feet to the ground. Then he was off to join one or more of his friends in Farmington.

Although he was a self-conscious lad of 15, John was not only doing a man's job and contributing considerably to the family income, but he was at the same time awakening to certain growing demands for self-gratification. Shouldn't he, as a normal adolescent, look for and find gratification now and seek adult responsibilities later? he wondered. Wasn't his life all askew somehow?

Such thoughts turned, tumbled, and churned in young John's mind as his hands continued their appointed task like those of an automaton. As he finished fashioning the fuse, the questions kept spinning aimlessly—hopelessly, it seemed. Was he simply self-determined? Self-contained? Self-absorbed? Or just plain selfish? He couldn't decide which. Perhaps he was guilty of them all.

John lit the fuse, then ran with all the speed his heavy-soled boots permitted. Within seconds the blasting powder would go off. If his clattering race with time did not take him at least fifty feet from the blast, there was a real danger of his being killed—either in the explosion by the ricocheting chunks from the vein, or by tons of coal crushing down upon him from the ceiling of the shaft.

With knuckles jammed against his ears, John made it to the shelter of a turn in the tunnel just as the blast went off.

For several seconds the roar echoed and reechoed; then intense silence followed once again. Did John say, "Thank

God!''? Probably not, but the phrase was there subconsciously, nevertheless.

As he walked to a nearby shaft where his jenny mule was tethered and led her to the coal car to fasten her chains for pulling the load, he began counting the days he had been spending as a human mole. He was simply working on working. That was it. Period!

Up there, outside the shaft, there was a blue sky, fluffy white clouds, fresh air, and the fragrance of flowers—not the odor of burnt gunpowder and smelly mules. A warm spring sun was shining, birds were singing, children were laughing and playing.

What am I doing down here? he asked himself. What am I contributing to the world? Is what I'm doing all that important?

He shook his head slowly. It may be important enough that someone needs to fill this job, but it needn't be me!

A good two tons of coal, loosened by the blast, lay piled not far from the car on the tracks. Nevertheless, he would still have to hurry in order to earn his four to five dollars a day. He had lost more time than he realized, occupied with his soliloquy.

The daily routine was broken only by the half-hour taken for lunch. Then the miners congregated in a wide space in the shaft to eat together and amuse themselves in rough dialogue common to them. Today John did not participate as he usually did. And in the future, as the hours telescoped imperceptibly one into another each day, he grew more and more reserved, retreating into himself, becoming more contemplative, more taciturn.

He did not confide his misgivings about his future in the mines to his father. There was not that kind of rapport between them—now or ever. Nor was there a feeling of special closeness between any of the members of the Shuler family. Each moved within his own little world of activity in a sterile, brittle, relationship more common among Old World immigrants than among the settled, homey generation of Americans they should have been.

But Providence undoubtedly had a hand in John's growing restlessness. The growing spark had been planted to help him rise above his mundane existence. For the present, however, he was confined to blundering attempts to find himself. At this moment he could not see the individual tree for the forest of questions and doubts that crowded in on him.

Meanwhile, back to work with his jenny for four or five loads of coal to be taken to the train of cars where it would be hauled to the surface and weighed. On each loaded car hung a large iron washer with his number printed on it. This made it simple for the weighmaster to keep track of each man's output and total his earnings for the day's work.

A miner raced against his own time and talent for bringing the most coal out of the mine. Frequently John's father assigned to him the job of picking up loose coal that constantly fell from the cars going to the cage and lay scattered along the tracks. He looked forward to this easier, quicker method of earning his fifty-six cents a ton, which was the only variation from his usual drilling and blasting routine.

But somewhere out there in the workaday world there was a better way of earning a living. He felt certain of it. What was it to be? How would he find it?

3

DETECTION

That June day in 1903 was bright and cheerful to most of Farmington's 1,500 population, for smog had yet to be invented, and all the smoke-belching refineries were miles away in the industrial cities of Illinois, Michigan, and Pennsylvania. Here the sky was blue, the air warm, and the breeze balmy with a faint fragrance of roses.

But John, returning home after a typical day spent in Farmington's number one coalpit, looked with unseeing eyes upon what to him was dull and faded. After all, what might one expect of a small mining town but drab red-brick store fronts, shops of rusted gray, mud-spattered hitching posts, and here and there, gas lamps sagging sadly in various directions?

John had left his father back in the mine to look after last-minute minutiae related to the Farmington Mine Union, for the senior Shuler headed the local chapter as president. Neither had he waited for friends who worked on the same shift to join him, although most of them lived in his neighborhood. Ordinarily, John—or "Buck" as his close friends dubbed him—was not a loner, but a laughing, fun-loving, outgoing lad who was as much at home with his pals as they were with him. Could it be that some mysterious inner spark had ignited in his brain, he wondered? What filled his mind with such questioning, such restlessness, such feelings of hopelessness?

With most of the male population of Farmington employed in the mines, no one gave him a second look, despite his black-as-his-shadow appearance that would have evoked laughter from onlookers and a trail of jeering small boys in almost any other town but Farmington. As it was, his looks fitted perfectly the mood he was in—black. Even the freight train, chugging dutifully from the mine entrance where it had taken on its load, failed to stop

John's stream of thought when it crossed Main Street, blocking his path.

The gondolas rattled slowly by on creaking rails. Perhaps the work he had done yesterday now helped heap high those hideous, coal-laden cars. Did it cross his mind how easy it would have been to hop aboard a gondola and ride out of town? Certainly his camouflage was right for it. No one would have caught the mere flash of the whites of his eyes had he been enthroned on one of those ebony mounds.

John watched the train until it had all but disappeared around a bend in the distance. Had he jumped aboard, would he have been able to shed his sooty, inane existence somewhere out there in the world beyond that he had never seen? Could his metamorphosis in any way resemble that of a seventeen-year locust? Could he—if given an opportunity—step out of this shell in which he was presently entrapped and begin some new experience of living, with wings to soar above all the humdrum of the present?

He sighed wistfully. Like the train that had disappeared down the track, his dream vanished into the reality of the moment. Then a voice cut into his reveries, and a hand was slapping him on the back.

"Hey, Buck, Old Boy." It was one of his buddies who had caught up with him. "Barney's got that keg of beer we chipped in on. Come on out to Todd's barn tonight, and we'll tie one on till the cows come home!"

The idea of having an evening with his friends turned John away from his gloom-laden mood. It was a perfect out for the present. All this distressing soul-searching could be relegated to a dark corner while he could bask in the sunshine of fun and forgetfulness.

With no other outlet for his disturbing thoughts, his spirits billowed like a balloon suddenly inflated with helium. His black mask split wide with a flashing display of white teeth.

"Man! T-t-that's g-g-g-great!" he stammered. Excitement always brought on that old plague—his stuttering habit. But at the moment it failed to deter him.

"It's j-j-just w-w-w-what I n-n-need. T-t-t-tell B-B-B-Barney I'll b-b-b-bring the c-c-cards!" he sputtered.

John loved playing cards almost as much as he liked drinking beer with his buddies—even when he was losing. Tonight he would have the opportunity he'd been waiting for to get even with Barney and win back what he'd lost in their last penny-ante game. It would take only a little luck, and right then, with his sudden reversal of spirit characteristic of his years, he was sure he would win the pot. The black cloud hanging so low over him for days had been set free like a kite in a gale with the string cut.

Before he left home that evening he told the truth about going to Barney's but omitted his plans for the escapade at Todd's barn. Nor did he make any promise as to what hour he would return. His parents knew that he knew how hard it was to get up early and get to work if he lost much sleep, so they left it up to him to keep sensible hours.

Actually, John didn't think his parents cared much what he did. He knew his father winked at activities he regarded as merely part of a teen-ager's growing-up process. As for his mother—he failed to note the sad-questioning look in her eyes when he went out the back door. Nor did he know that she would lie awake far into the early-morning hours after she had found what he had left in his dirty miner's coat pocket after his bath. She didn't find them until after he had gone, and the questions they left unanswered kept her staring into the darkness until she heard him stumbling into his room. Only then did she fall into troubled sleep.

Ordinarily, Mother Shuler trusted her son to keep respectable hours and to stay out of trouble. But that evening, in his haste to get away with the boys, John hadn't taken time to empty his coat pockets as he usually did when he took his bath. And that afternoon he had bought a fresh deck of cards and had forgotten to throw away the old pack. Worst of all, he had left a .32-caliber pistol in his coat.

When confronted by his mother at breakfast, John's blush turned several shades of red at her outburst.

"John Lewis! What is the meaning of this gun I found in your pocket?" she demanded in a stern voice that cracked under the strain. She was teetering the gleaming, nickel-plated pistol on her index finger as though it might suddenly go off.

The rest of the family stared at him in wide-eyed astonishment. His brothers and sisters bombarded him with questions from all sides. He had never seen them take such a sudden interest in him.

It was obvious that even his father had not been told about the gun, for he dropped his spoon in his cereal and looked open-mouthed from the pistol to his son in startled silence.

That was when his brothers and sisters took over the inquisition, asking (or stating) what they suspected: He was a burglar, a highway robber, a purse snatcher—maybe he had even *killed* somebody! His first impulse was to revert to what he might have done when he was in grade school, before he had begun work in the mines as a man—to run upstairs and shut himself in his room until things had quieted down.

Father Shuler's sudden recovery of his voice brought John quickly to manhood in his thinking. At first Mr. Shuler blushed as deeply as his son before his face drained to a white heat of anger. Then his bellow put to silence the childish babble. When he spoke again, however, it was almost in a hoarse whisper from compressed lips:

"John Lewis Shuler! You heard your mother! *Explain yourself!*"

The boy shrank down in his chair until he seemed almost the sitting height of his younger brother Roy. Then he began to stammer and stutter in abject confusion. It took some time before his family—even though they were familiar with his hesitant expression under normal conditions—could grasp his explanation.

That was when they learned that his gang had aped William Tell in using small rifles to knock ashes off each other's cigarettes. He told how they had begun lengthening the distance between the rifle and the target until they had become apprehensive about the risk they were taking. He explained that he had bought the pistol through a Sears, Roebuck catalog. He had had no specific plans for using it. He simply thought it smart to have a pistol in his pocket. It was just as well he had forgotten to take it with him, what with all of the beer drinking they had done. One of those empty heads might have suggested using it instead of a rifle to knock off their cigarette ashes. There was no telling what the outcome might have been.

The silence was almost deafening when the inquisition about

the revolver was over. But a faint smile tugged at the corner of his father's mouth when Mother Shuler began questioning him about the deck of well-worn cards she had also found in his pocket. His father knew John played poker and took his side on that point, explaining that this was all part of growing up. He made it clear that this was not to be held against the boy.

From that day on, however, Mother Shuler tried to be more observant of her son's moods, even though she had little time to spend with him. She had never questioned the obvious pedestal upon which he placed his father until she learned that her husband regarded playing poker as beneficial for the boy. Then she began to doubt that all of his father's influence was for the best. It was from that point that she kept her eyes open, watching for an opportunity to express herself on his behalf.

Nearly a year passed before the opportunity came when she thought she might be of some real help to her son. Even then she hesitated to express her wishes because it was on the touchy subject of religion. In that area she herself lacked conviction, because she had given up churchgoing when she had left England at the age of 16. At that time she had come to the States and married John's father. She hadn't attended church since and was hardly in a position to suggest that her eldest son do so. But when she felt the right opportunity presented itself, she did. In later years even she had to admit that the events that followed her efforts were positively providential; the changes that took place in the life of John Lewis were nothing short of miraculous.

4

IDEALIZATION

No one—least of all Mother Shuler—could have had the remotest idea that it would be a professional baseball star who would be the commanding influence in shaping the future of her son, redirecting his interests, and introducing an abrupt about-face in the lenient life style of the teen-ager.

John Lewis had enjoyed playing ball during his grade-school years, yet he was anything but a baseball fan. He knew nothing of batting averages, nor of the outstanding member of the Chicago, Pittsburgh, and Philadelphia teams who had beaten Ty Cobb's record: 98 bases stolen in 150 games. This record breaker had stolen 98 bases in 116 games and was the first man in baseball history to circle the diamond from a standing start in 14 seconds flat. His peak batting average was .356 with the Chicago White Stockings.

Billy Sunday was the name of that ball player who was destined to make an even greater name for himself as a sawdust trail revivalist. The events in the life of that barnstormer for God have been told and retold since the day he retired from baseball and took up his career as an evangelist at the age of 34. His second rise to fame was not as meteoric as it had been in baseball. He began to develop his style of campaigning in many Midwestern small towns before his international reputation as a speaker started snowballing.

It was one of those providential events in Sunday's early years, so important to John Shuler, that the evangelist's promoters chose Farmington as a test town before concentrating on big cities such as Chicago, Philadelphia, and New York, where his audiences would number into the thousands. Perhaps they wanted to see how effective Sunday's effort would be in a small community of rough, uneducated miners who were anything but active Christians—despite the fact that there were five denominations struggling to support churches in the area. Attendance was thin in all of them; the attitude of the Shulers toward religion was typical of the general population.

Fred Fischer, Sunday's gospel singer and music director, was a large, handsome man with a walrus mustache and wavy hair who always wore high stiff collars and a pince-nez. Although actually untrained as a singer or choir leader, the press usually spoke of his "musical direction" as "a grand success."

"Mr. Fischer," as Billy always referred to him, had a certain flair that attracted the public eye. Under his direction, the lively gospel tunes caught the ear of many casual passers-by, lured them into the evangelist's sawdust-padded tent, and chained them to the folding benches until Billy electrified them with his unique, soul-inspiring messages.

Billy Sunday's technique was remarkably successful, despite the fact that he confessed he was anything but an elocutionist. He once told a friend that he "wouldn't know a rule of syntax if it came walking down the middle of the road!" What grabbed the attention of his listeners from the moment he opened his mouth (with volume such as one associated with sports stadiums rather than church podiums) was his short, staccato sentences that hit his listeners like straight blows from the shoulder.

Sunday pounded home his arguments for turning from sin and serving God in down-to-earth, everyday language that even a child could understand. His sound reasoning indelibly impressed the minds of every audience he addressed. Rodeheaver, who was to spend more than thirty years with Sunday and later authored his biography, captured the evangelist's success best in one sentence: "People came to appraise Billy Sunday; they remained to praise God!"

Often Sunday told his audiences of his early life as a physical weakling and how right habits of living, with development of a good workout routine at the YMCA, had turned him into a star athlete. His listeners saw a man in perfect physical condition, his well-cut suits accenting his slim, athletic figure. One University of Pennsylvania student described how Billy appealed to young people at a campus assembly program:

"He appeared to me to be a man in every way," he wrote. "By his sheer personality he made me strive to be all that is best in manhood."

The afternoon that Billy Sunday's work crew arrived in Farmington, John Shuler happened to see the teams of horses turning into the town park, bringing in wagons piled high with canvas, poles, stakes, and other paraphernalia ordinarily associated with traveling circuses and sideshows. It was only natural for him to surmise that was what this was to be. But when he asked one of the workmen what circus he was with, he was surprised at the man's reply.

This was no circus or sideshow, he was told. From the laconic information the man gave in between blows delivered upon a tent stake with a heavy-headed mallet, he got the impression it was some kind of chautauqua. When he asked who the speaker would be, the man had grunted, "Billy Sunday." John turned on his heel to walk away.

"Never heard of him!" he sniffed.

The workman's blow seemed to stall in midair. It fell short of the stake, and the worker's eyes met John's for the first time.

"Ya neva heered tell of Billy Sunday?" he croaked incredulously.

"N-n-n-no, n-n-n-nev-ver!" John stammered sheepishly, color beginning to rise in his cheeks.

"Wahl," the worker drawled, "ya wahl, son, ya wahl!"

Avoiding the glances he got from the crowd of onlookers now gathering, his blush deepening, John elbowed his way into the street and began walking home. The quizzical arch of his eyebrows lowered into a slight frown. It was a disappointment not to have some excitement to look forward to, since there was so little in the way of entertainment in Farmington or any nearby towns. But even though chautauquas had been popular for the past quarter century, they had begun to dim in their appeal—especially to the younger set.

John dismissed the incident from his mind and began consoling himself with the plans that he and his buddies had begun making for the construction of their own private swimming hole down at the bend in the creek. There would be a lot of work to be done to deepen the channel and pile up a rock dam high enough to make it safe for diving and the stunting that they looked forward to. Meanwhile, however, until more of the boys could get together at the same time, there wasn't much he could do by himself.

Mother Shuler was just pulling a pan of golden-brown biscuits from the oven as John came in the back door.

"Ummm!" he mumbled. "Do they ever smell good! I'm ready for supper right now!" But glancing at the big oaken clock on the wall, cheerfully tick-tocking the afternoon away, he noted it would be another twenty minutes before suppertime.

"We could eat early tonight if your father was home. Everything's ready," she said, putting the biscuits back into the warming oven.

The house was unusually quiet, and he asked where the rest of the family was.

"They're all over at the Morrisons' helping Timmy celebrate his tenth birthday. They'll be so full of Mrs. Morrison's ice cream and chocolate cake that they probably won't want any supper. We won't wait for them," she sighed, sitting down for a moment's rest before setting the table.

She looked up at her son, still standing by the door. Her clear, dark eyes thoughtfully appraised him as if for the first time. It wasn't that he had grown up so quickly that she had hardly noticed his physical maturing. It was the inner John Lewis that she scarcely knew. She seldom had time for more than a few words with him, and then it was only to ask him to bring in an extra armload of wood when his younger brothers, Roy and Louis, forgot to, or to inquire whether he was getting enough food in the lunchpail she packed for him to take to the mine. There never seemed any meaningful contact between them.

John, too, sensing the inadequacy of their communication, pulled up a footstool the younger children used to reach the cupboards and sat at her feet, looking up into her broad features that were so much like his own.

Having already dismissed from his thoughts what he regarded as an inconsequential brush with the Billy Sunday venture coming to Farmington, the only subject fresh in his mind was his plans for the swimming hole.

"Sure hope Barney and I and the rest of the gang can get in some real s-s-s-swimming this s-s-s-summer," he began, having trouble with his *s*'s despite his relaxation. "I think it's going to be hotter than ever." He wiped a few drops of moisture from his forehead with the back of his hand.

Mother Shuler fondly patted his head and brushed back his thick, black locks. It was only the heat of the baking oven in the kitchen that made it so warm, but in an effort to draw him out and get him to talk more she asked, teasingly, "You planning to spend time at the Mississippi? Maybe you can swim across it with your father." She pursed her lips, trying not to smile while attempting to joke with him, yet realizing there was nothing he'd rather do than have the prowess of his father in being able to swim that mile-wide current.

"Oh, no!" John's quick response surprised her. "We're going to dam up the creek and make a big swimming hole. It'll be real handy. We can jump in on our way home from the mine and save a lot of scrub-up time."

"Is there that much water in the creek during the summer? Where's the dam going to be?"

Practical mother, as she always was, John was thinking. He might as well tell her the details. So before he could evaluate what her opinion of the plan might be, he had told all about putting the dam down at the widest point of the creek on old man Johnson's property.

"Oh?" her expression showing unexpected interest. "And what does Mr. Johnson think about your doing this on his land?"

"He won't care. He doesn't use his south forty for anything anymore."

"You mean you boys haven't even *asked* his permission?"

"N-n-n-no," John faltered. "Y-y-y-you t-t-t-think we s-s-s-s-sh-sh-should?" His stuttering suddenly returned when he realized the implication—that he hadn't shown mature judgment in the matter.

"Why of course you should, John!" Her tone was emphatic. "How do you know he doesn't plan to divert the creek to irrigate the watermelons he sometimes grows down there? Maybe it's too late for them, but just right for pumpkins, or something else."

John might have admitted there was a slight possibility, but his father's coming home just then brought their conversation to an end. The two of them took turns washing up for supper. There was no other sound except the clink of spoons being placed in the covered dishes mother brought to the table, and the scraping of their chairs being pulled under the table as they sat down.

There were only the three of them, and it was unusually quiet without the children present. John was so absorbed in the new complication about building the swimming hole without permission that he hardly heard his father mention having seen the big tent go up downtown. He, too, had surmised that it was another circus come to town.

John's ears pricked up at that point, and he volunteered what he had learned it was to be—a Billy Sunday chautauqua.

"Billy Sunday?" his father queried sharply. "Not *the* Billy Sunday who used to play with Chicago?" He helped himself to another of his wife's delicious biscuits, spreading it with butter and honey while he looked expectantly at his son.

John shook his head, admitting he didn't know, that he'd never heard of anybody by the name of Billy Sunday who did anything. But if he *were* a big baseball star, what would he be doing coming to Farmington? he wondered aloud.

It was a good question, Father Shuler agreed. "You'd make a good lawyer, John. That's sound deduction."

The subject was dropped after father mentioned hearing some of the more sports-minded men at the mine talk about Sunday's batting average and how he could whiz around the bases in nothing flat. Surely he wouldn't be coming to town and putting up a tent to brag about it, though, would he?

It was hardly likely. They would soon find out. In a little burg like Farmington the news of what it was all about would spread quickly enough, of that they could be certain.

5

CONFRONTATION

When John, Barney, and five others of the gang finally got together to begin work on the dam, they met on the creek bank, below the Johnson farm. The hay barn stood between them and the Johnson house, and both were some distance up the hill so they were well out of earshot.

"Well, what're we waitin' for?" one of the boys exclaimed impatiently.

Reluctantly, acting as spokesman, Barney explained that Buck had brought up the matter of getting old man Johnson's permission before they started work on the dam. The response was immediate defiance. No one except John thought it was necessary. But he was adamant, impressed as he was that his mother had been right in her sensible insistence that it was the only course to take.

"All right, Buck," Barney exploded, "if you're so sure it's gotta be done, you're the one to do it!"

There was instant agreement, with each boy's voice chiming in noisily, backing Barney. But John shook his head stolidly.

"Oh, no, you don't! You're not going to make any martyr out of me—not after I got caught hoisting those buckets of maple sap through old man Johnson's fence that we collected from his trees last spring! Who got the blame for that? Me! That's who! You think he'd give me the time of day after that? Fat chance he'd go granting any favor I'd ask!"

There was a murmur of awful admission that John had a point. The chore was batted back and forth from one boy to another, with each member of the gang disavowing any intention of setting foot on Johnson's doorstep to try to get his permission for the project. The result was unavoidable. The discussion ground to an agonizing halt, and the project died a painful death right then and there. Mournfully, each boy shouldered his shovel and headed for home.

In the weeks that followed, news spread about Billy Sunday's tent meetings in town. The miners who had attended discussed him during their lunch periods, and housewives gossiped about it over their back-yard fences. Opinions were unanimous: as a preacher he far surpassed every other minister in any one of the churches. His messages were appealingly fresh, his delivery striking, and his personal appearance in a faultlessly pressed suit as he agilely sprang from one side of the speaker's podium to the other was something worth seeing.

Possibly more men were attracted by his fine physical build than were women; but even that was debatable. And many a young woman failed to miss a night after once being thrilled by that "divine" song leader, Fred Fischer. Many of the new songs they sang caught on immediately and are still being sung today.

Surprisingly, Sunday's subjects were remembered and discussed at length. He made a point of emphasizing, when he made his appeals to "come forward," that the doctrine of growing in grace, of holding that conversion was only the first step in working out a Christian's salvation, was not as important as "hitting the trail" for total commitment.

The weeks went by quickly in Sunday's six-week campaign. The Shulers even broke their mealtime silence more than once to discuss what they had heard about the meetings. Mother Shuler repeated what a neighbor had told her, that it was impossible for anyone to become a real and useful Christian unless one was willing to do the things that are absolutely essential to spiritual growth.

"What does all that mean?" Father Shuler demanded.

"Well, the way Lucy explained it," Mrs. Shuler replied, "Billy Sunday said it was necessary to read the Bible, pray, win souls, *shun evil companions* (she paused to look over at John Lewis significantly), join a church, and give to support the Lord's work."

"Sounds about right to me," Father Shuler commented laconically.

But why none of the Shuler family ever made a move to go to hear Billy Sunday remains a mystery. Perhaps Mother Shuler was too tired after a long day of caring for her family, with all the baking, washing, meal planning, mending, cleaning house, and helping the children with their chores. She had an excuse if any of them did. Then, too, not being one to go out often, she might have thought she did not have the wardrobe expected of a respectable woman who represented the Shuler family.

The one positive aspect during those weeks was that she kept after John to go to the meetings, hoping, no doubt, that they would spark his interest in spiritual things. Night after night she asked her son why he didn't go, that after all, Billy Sunday had been a great baseball player, and it wouldn't hurt to go see what a star looked like. She felt sure her John would learn something more inspiring than simply spending another night playing poker with his pals.

"Yes, Mother," John Lewis smiled back indulgently each time she prodded him.

"Maybe I'll go one of these nights," he promised. But each time his fingers were crossed, and he really hadn't the slightest intention of going. He just wanted to please her. His father had no interest in religion whatever, and he had to admit he was of the same frame of mind.

The last night of the Sunday series rolled around, and, as it happened, only three of the gang turned up at their usual meeting place. Poker playing somehow had lost its appeal, and their fun barrel had become as dry as their beer keg. What were they to do for amusement? That was when someone suggested they go down to see what Billy Sunday had to say. Not one of their group had gone before, but they had to admit that everyone who had spoken to them about the great sportsman-turned-sky-pilot reported that he had been great. Why not look in on him? After all, it *was* his last night. It would be their only chance to see what he looked like.

John Lewis, not to be persuaded, told them to go if they wanted to, but he wasn't about to listen to any tear-jerker and sit through all those mournful hymns. He was all out for fun but was not about to sink to the depths of going to that kind of meeting just to find amusement in berating someone's silly religious experience.

"Go if you want to," John stated solemnly, "but I'm going

home. None of that sob-sister stuff for me!"

"Whatcha' got better to do, Buck?" one of the gang asked.

It was a long shot, but it worked. John had to admit there wasn't anything to do, so reluctantly he agreed to tag along.

The four of them arrived just as the singing began, and they found seats near the back where they could slip in or out unobtrusively.

They looked at one another significantly, mouths turned down but smiles twitching at the corners, sheepishly cognizant of the fact that the music appealed to them, even if they didn't join in the singing. But when Billy Sunday stood up to speak, they sat up rigidly in their seats, straining to get a better look at the man. They were surprised that he wasn't taller, his having grown in their imaginations each time they had heard others tell about him. Actually, he was a little shorter than John, and had John's coloring of hair and eyes. But his build was even better than John's father's, even though his shoulders were not quite as broad and he did not give evidence of having huge biceps like the senior Shuler.

However, from the moment Billy Sunday opened his mouth he got John's undivided attention. John was never to forget the evangelist's opening text taken from the Gospel of Mark, chapter 12, verse 34: "Thou art not far from the kingdom of God." It was such a strange thought, it seemed to John. Could he relate it in any way to his own earnest search for a more meaningful existence during the past year? Of course Sunday was thinking of those who had been attending his meetings every night and were almost persuaded to make their commitment to God. He hoped that they were near the kingdom and would step over the line when he would make his final appeal.

That night Billy Sunday apparently was out to answer all the questions that had been making the rounds about him—remarkably enough, even the unspoken ones John Lewis had in mind. He answered their criticism about his slangy language; their unkind comments about his not being much of a man to give up baseball for religion; and the comparison they made of him with their hometown pastors. His replies were bluntly to the point:

"I don't use much high-falutin' language," he admitted. "I learned years ago to put the cookies and jam on the lowest shelf."

As to barbs about his manhood, he countered, "You can't measure manhood with a tapeline around your biceps! Let me tell you, the manliest man is the man who will acknowledge Jesus Christ."

Then turning to look squarely into the eyes of one local minister, he attempted to speak kindly, yet frankly: "I drive the same kind of nails all orthodox preachers do. The only difference is that they use a *tack* hammer and I use a *sledge!*"

The crowd gasped, grinned at one another, and applauded loudly. After a pause he continued with his sermon. One part of it bored into John Lewis' heart: "Morality doesn't save anybody. Your culture doesn't save you. I don't care who you are or how good you are; if you reject Jesus Christ, you are doomed. God hasn't one plan of salvation for the millionaire and another for the hobo. He has the same plan for everybody. God isn't going to ask *you* whether you like it or not, either. He isn't going to ask you your opinion of His plan. There it is, and we'll have to take it as God gives it." Billy stepped out in front of the podium and, holding high his Bible with one hand and pointing to it with the other, continued: "Before I was converted I could go five rounds so fast you couldn't see me for the dust, and I'm still pretty handy with my dukes and I can still deliver the goods with all express charges prepaid. Before I was converted I could run one hundred yards in ten seconds and circle the bases in fourteen seconds—and I could run just as fast after I was converted. So you don't have to be a dishrag proposition at all to be a Christian."

His words, flung like darts in all directions, hit hearts everywhere. They found their mark in John Lewis, stinging him, thrilling him, humbling him. But the evangelist's accusations had only begun to warm up. He jogged rapidly to one end of the platform, then back to the other, all heads turning to follow him, wondering what to expect next. He paused and began to speak softly and earnestly, but gradually building up his crescendo.

"Listen, my friends," he almost whispered, "when a man starts on a journey, he has one object in view—the end. A journey is well—if it ends well. We are all on a journey to eternity. What will be the end? God doesn't care what your present position in life is. God doesn't care about that. What shall the end be?" he shouted. "When pleasures pass away and sorrow and weeping take their place, *what shall the end be?*"

John Lewis and his pals sat like stone figures with eyes riveted on Billy Sunday as he wound up his final appeal to the people of Farmington:

"You can be a Christian if you want to, and it is your cussedness that you are unwilling to give up what keeps you away from God. Don't tell God that you can't. Just say that you don't want to be a Christian; that's the way to be a man. Just say I don't want to be decent. I don't want to quit cussing. I don't want to quit booze. I don't want to quit lying. If I should be a Christian I would have to quit all these things and I don't want to do it. Tell God you are not man enough to be a Christian. Don't try to saddle it off on the Lord. You don't want to do it, that's all; that's the trouble with you!"

The final words Billy used to close his appeal were lost on John Lewis. He had already made up his mind that if Sunday made a call for people to make their stand to be Christians, he would go up and give him his hand.

Billy Sunday made the call to hit the sawdust trail, and John Lewis and his pals were among the first of those who crowded to the front. None of the boys could believe it was happening to them, but they were so caught up in the magic of the moment that they scarcely knew how they got there. Then they were shaking hands with Billy Sunday himself, hearing him say fervently to each one, "God bless you, son!"

6

TRANSFORMATION

Four momentous happenings occurred the night John Lewis went to hear Billy Sunday, each culminating at just the right juncture to bring about his complete spiritual metamorphosis. He left the tent physically the same as he had entered it, but the inner man was no longer the same—nor was he ever again to be the same. He himself could not for the life of him explain the change that had taken place. All he was conscious of was that although there were still many ties to his old life, none of them were really binding.

Event number one was that electrifying moment when he gave his hand to Billy Sunday signifying his promise to become a Christian. There were deeper implications in that simple handclasp than he knew, John thought later. In subsequent years he felt as though something was exchanged between them. The rapport John had felt in that brief physical and mental contact with the evangelist was never to dim as long as he lived. Actually, although the two were never to meet again, Sunday's influence—consciously or unconsciously—grew more significant with the passing years. It was almost as if something of his mantle had fallen on John, as Elijah's mantle fell on Elisha.

The second major turn of events came when John was asked to sign a card indicating his denominational preference. Did he wish to join the Baptist, Methodist, Presbyterian, Congregational, or Episcopal Church? John was stumped until he suddenly recalled that his mother had once told him she had attended a Methodist church in England before she immigrated to America. So it was by this odd quirk—also undeniably providential, as it was later to turn out—that he aligned himself with the Methodists.

Event number three was instrumental in helping him crystallize the step into Christianity he had taken when a small booklet was handed each penitent who had come down the sawdust trail on that never-to-be-forgotten summer evening in Farmington, Illinois. In it John read, "By this act of coming forward publicly, you have acknowledged your faith in Jesus Christ as your personal Saviour; and since this was the sole requirement of salvation or rebirth, you may know on the authority of God's Word that you are now a child of God (John 1:12). It is impossible for you to become a useful Christian unless you are willing to do the things that are absolutely essential to your spiritual strength—pray, win souls, shun evil companions, join a church, and give toward the support of the Lord's work."

The remainder of the instructions gave the new believer the impression that once he had shaken Sunday's hand, he had done all that was necessary to claim his mansion in heaven. With this shortsighted transaction, one's relationship with God was supposedly complete, the contract filled and forever concluded.

Event number four was the most significant of all—entailing as it did the relationship he was to enter into from then on with his heavenly Father. The first point given in the instruction booklet was that he was to pray. Just how he was to go about this he hadn't the slightest idea. All he was certain of was that people knelt when they prayed, so that was the first thing he did when he returned to his room that night.

The house was in darkness; all the members of the family were asleep. So he simply got down on his knees beside his bed and in the stillness talked to God for the first time in his life. He frankly told the Lord all about himself, about how he had questioned the trend of his life for a long time, and he sincerely asked for help and guidance in living in this new way that had been so graphically pointed out to him for the first time. He told God he needed to be shown the way to make the changes he knew would be necessary. All he could ask for was that divine guidance be given him, that his understanding would be increased so he would know how to live day by day. He thanked God again and again for the new peace and contentment that had come to him. Finally he fell asleep, happier than he'd ever been, knowing that a new life, with undreamed-of possibilities, was opening before him.

At breakfast next morning both Father and Mother Shuler

caught the new spark of joy in their son's eyes, and he couldn't help giving them a synopsis of his experience the night before. However, his true feelings were as yet too new and too sacred to discuss in any detail. He did mention that he had stated his preference for the Methodists and that he would probably be attending services at the Methodist church the following Sunday.

His mother was of course elated at this unexpected but longed-for turn of events and expressed her happiness for her son's having actually taken a stand for the church of her choice. The response of his father surprised them both. He did not belittle John's sudden interest in religion; instead he chided him about his choice of churches.

"Why didn't you write *Presbyterian* on your card? At least they are people with money and prestige, and far ahead of these Methodists!" he said, giving his wife a sly look.

"Why, John Shuler," she addressed her husband, "I'll have you know that back where I came from in England, the Methodists were the most respected people in town! As far as money is concerned, that has little to do with membership in any church!"

Mother Shuler patted John Lewis on the shoulder approvingly and ended their brief dialogue by handing them both their lunch boxes, as she commented, "You made a wise choice, son. I'm so happy for you!"

Just as they were leaving, John Lewis turned to ask, "Mother, do we have a Bible? My new commitment calls for Bible study, and as ignorant as I am about anything in it, I'm going to have to do some studying."

"Yes, I think I have one I brought with me from England. It may be in my trunk somewhere. I'll find it today so you can have it when you get home," she replied happily, wiping the corner of her eye with her apron.

That day John Lewis was as deep in thought as he was deep in the mine, reviewing what had happened to him, trying to understand the belief and sudden faith that had welled up within him. His decision had been aided by Billy Sunday but not forced by him. John had groped for God in the darkness of his ignorance. Now he was simply begging God for enlightenment and that he would be used of God in any way that would bring purpose into his life. He knew that the night before, while he was on his knees, the door had swung open wide for him. There had been no voice from heaven, no fiery finger pointing the way, no thunder and lightning; only a still small voice had spoken to his heart. Now he was waiting to be led by God in the way he should go.

At noon, when he went to eat his lunch with the rest of the men, he got to talk with two of his gang who had been with him and had also taken their stand to be Christians. They were strangely quiet and obviously embarrassed about the whole incident. They, like many another sawdust trail "convert," had been swayed by the dramatics and popular emotion of the moment. If they had experienced a softening of their hearts and had made an inward promise to change their lives, their attitude now indicated that they regretted their rashness. Their replies to John's questions about what difference their decision would make in their lives were strangely garbled and lost in meaningless mumbling as they munched their sandwiches.

John was baffled by their unusual aloofness. They seemed to be watching him quizzically, as though he had become irrational, as though he might suddenly become violent—especially when he mentioned being so glad that God had come into his heart and was going to help him do something with his life. He, in turn, became silent and introspective and left them to their own thoughts. How, he wondered, had this wonderful experience come to *him* and not to his buddies? Only God knew.

Working in the coalpit that afternoon, he no longer felt alone. John knew he had a heavenly Father who was aware he was seeking Him with all his heart, and he whispered fervently, "Here I am, Lord. Lead me, do what You want with me, but stay with me, Lord, and never leave me." Tears traced white rivulets down his blackened cheeks. But they were tears of happiness, not of regret. The boy who had returned to the mine was not the same one who had been there the day before, nor was he ever to be the same again.

Back in his room that night, he began reading the Bible his mother, not finding her own, had bought for him. As with other books he had read at school, he began at the beginning and became familiar with Biblical history and God's leading in the lives of the prophets and the children of Israel. He was touched by their trials but incensed at their foolish blindness in not recognizing the direct and visible leading of God through the Red Sea and by the pillar of cloud.

Before he went to bed he reviewed in Billy Sunday's booklet the pledge he had taken. So far he was doing what he had been admonished to do: he was praying and reading the Bible. But what was he going to do with those parts about "winning souls" and "shunning evil companions"? He had tried to speak to the two members of his gang about their religious experience, but had been rebuffed. And what was he going to do the next time a poker party was set up? He wouldn't go, of course. He couldn't go. He didn't want to go, somehow. The appeal was gone. But how could he cut himself off from all his old acquaintances and still do something to influence them to try a better way of living, and to seek God's direction? That proved to be a part of the puzzle that would take some time to work out.

Meanwhile, he began attending the Methodist Sunday school and joined a class of twenty young men taught by an earnest Christian woman. He was told he would soon be asked whether he wished to be immersed or sprinkled when he became a member of the church.

That led to some serious Bible study, and John came to the conclusion that John the Baptist had held his efforts where "there was much water" and that he had baptized Jesus in the River Jordan. In his endeavor to follow in the footsteps of the Saviour, John Lewis chose immersion. He could not understand how sprinkling a few drops of water on a person's head was in line with Paul's observation that the Colossian Christians had been *"buried with Him [Jesus] in baptism"* (Col. 2:12).

Nevertheless, some of the group joining the church at the time John did chose to be sprinkled. John and a few others who had also decided to be immersed were taken by the pastor to a nearby creek for the Biblical rite. There were no baptismal robes, so each candidate came in whatever he or she wanted to wear into the water. Afterward they walked to their homes, going half a mile or more in their wet clothing. Only the women brought long coats to cover their wetness when they walked from the creek.

John anticipated a warm reception as a new church member by his Sunday school teacher the following week, but was disappointed to find her absent. There was concern about her health because he was told she had never been absent before. However, the man who took her place proved to be unforgettable, since the subject he discussed caused John to leave the Methodist Church.

INTERMISSION

With Billy Sunday's meetings over, the tent pulled down, and the park raked clean of sawdust and shavings, the citizens of Farmington settled themselves to endure a quiet summer. Perhaps there would be a few community picnics, a band concert on the Fourth of July with fireworks, or a performance or two by some traveling entertainer, but this was about the extent of excitement they could hope for to break the monotony.

However, something—or rather someone—chose this time of all times to plan his own private religious campaign for the sleepy little mining town. He was one of those industrious lay workers for a religious publishing house who were then known as colporteurs. His intentions were good. He probably thought he might be instrumental in capitalizing on Billy Sunday's campaign by bringing these people some good religious reading material to help them in their new-found Christian experience. But for reasons he failed to understand, up to this Friday afternoon not a soul had taken kindly to him.

Wendall Benson, a stout, round-cheeked young ministerial student working his way through college, was one of those characters who helped give credence to that age-old belief that all fat men are jolly. Actually, it was generally true of Wendall, too. However, that first day he spent in Farmington had been enough to try the soul of a saint. He had walked untold miles up and down the best areas of town and had even hiked out to a few outlying farms without getting more than a few curt words from housewives or worse from sleepy miners whom he had gotten out of bed to answer his knock at their doors.

Not even once had he had the opportunity to open his prospectus. In fact, he had been given to understand more than

once that Farmington had had about all the religion it could stand
that summer as a result of Billy Sunday and the subsequent drive
the preachers of five churches were now holding to increase the
number of their flocks. The miners he had awakened were, it
seemed, all on the graveyard shift, with wives who were either out
back washing or over at a neighbor's—at least they weren't there to
intercept Benson's intrusion on their slumbers. This fact none
bothered to explain. They simply bid the poor order taker begone
before they sicked their dogs on him, all but turning the air purple
with their expletive explosions.

It was late that Friday afternoon, and long past his usual Friday
quitting time, when Benson reached the last house on the block
that he had been working so disheartedly. His courage down to the
level of his dusty shoe tops, he was dragging one weary foot after
another, shifting his prospectus satchel from hand to hand, the
weight bringing one shoulder down to the level the other had
sagged to a moment before. He closed his eyes for a silent, fervent
prayer, laying it on the line with the Lord, telling Him how he felt
about colporteuring. He believed it to be *His* work, but he was
having so little proof of it that day. Could he be forgiven if he was
beginning to have doubts?

Benson opened his tear-blurred blue eyes just in time to avoid
butting his head against a rural mailbox directly in front of him. It
bore the name *A. Gent* and stood sentinel before a white picket gate
opening into a long graveled walk leading to a small house at the
rear of a deep, narrow lot. Not much of a prospect, he thought. He
hesitated to open the gate, trusting his usual reliable sense that
there was a dog in the yard, even if he couldn't see one. Would it
be worth the risk, or even the effort, to walk that far just to get
another rebuff to match all the others he'd received that day?

"Dear Lord," he prayed in a hoarse whisper, his hand on the
latch, "if this is truly Your work, won't You give me a sign? You
know how I've worked all day without a single word of
encouragement, and this is the last house I'll canvass today. If
You're in this work, please let me get just one small order from the
people who live here. I'm not asking too much, am I? After all, I
think it no more than right that You give me a *little* encouragement!"

Wendall gave a deep sigh as he glanced once more at the mailbox. Maybe the name was a good omen. If the man who lived here was truly *a gent* as the name suggested, at least he'd be treated courteously. Furtively opening the gate, he took a step inside. So far, so good. No dog appeared. He tiptoed down the brown graveled path, trying not to make the slightest grating sound—just in case!

He had just reached the first step up to the porch when he caught sight of a scarecrow of a man bounding toward the screen door to meet him.

"Man alive!" the thin one exclaimed, "how'd you ever get up the walk without my boxer taking a leg off you? He *never* lets anyone get inside the gate unless I call him off!"

"Oh, that so?" Wendall asked, looking around furtively—still unsure of his safety. Then, beaming good-naturedly up at his prospect, he admitted he was thankful for being overlooked.

"Dogs seem to take to me everywhere I go," he explained, smiling ruefully, pulling one pant leg up far enough to reveal several white scars and one so recent it was still red.

"Mr. Gent, I'm Wendall Benson, representative of the Battle Creek Publishing House up in the State of Michigan, and I have some outstanding new books I'd like to show you. Could I come in for a min—?"

Wendall broke off, sensing from Gent's face another turn-down. Icicles seemed to be forming around his heart, so fearful was he of facing failure again.

"No," Gent said faintly, "not now, at least. My wife's away tonight visiting relatives, and I'm busy getting my own supper. Could you come back in about an hour or so?"

"No, I'm afraid not, Mr. Gent. You see—" He was about to say he was a Seventh-day Adventist and that all his work had to be done before sundown, but he didn't, knowing full well how most people reacted to those of his faith. He felt the admission would destroy any possibility of a sale then and there.

But the scrawny little man who ordinarily was not very observant caught the beaten look that had crept over the younger man's face. Benson had taken his foot off the porch step and was already turning to leave.

"Say!" Gent exclaimed so suddenly he surprised even himself, "why don't you come on in anyway and have a snack with me? I'll be glad for a little company. You won't get much, but you're welcome to what I've got. You can rest up while we eat, then you can show me your books." Gent unhooked the screen door and opened it wide in invitation. "Come on in, Mr.——"

"Benson. Wendall Benson. It surely is neighborly of you to ask me to supper. I do appreciate your kindness!" Benson's pudgy face beamed happily, turning slightly pink in anticipation as he was ushered into the house and shown a comfortable easy chair.

"I'll be ready in just a few minutes," Gent promised, disappearing into the adjoining room.

Benson breathed a soulful sigh of thanks to God for this much sympathy and for the opportunity to get off his aching feet. He looked around the plain little parlor and was pleasantly surprised to find a fairly sizable collection of books in a glass case. Among the volumes a large old family Bible stood out—certainly a good sign, he told himself. A surge of hopefulness flowed in his breast, which he sought valiantly to quell before he got carried away with happiness. There was no use getting set up for another big letdown. As promising as Gent seemed, he could easily be another dud.

"Please, dear God," Benson whispered, *"don't* let him be!"

Gent's hospitality turned out to be a rather slim meal of his wife's leftovers. Nevertheless, after Benson had been invited to freshen up and grace had been said, they both thoroughly enjoyed their camaraderie while polishing off the simple fare together.

As they chatted amiably, comparing notes on their interests, Benson learned, with another slight lift of spirit, that Gent was an active deacon in the nearby Methodist church. Often, Gent stated, he was called upon to take Sunday school classes, being a relief teacher when one of the regulars was absent.

With the meal over and the dishes cleared away, they remained at the table while Wendall brought out his prospectus containing choice portions of the books for which he was taking orders.

Gent's immediate interest was gratifying. He admitted that any or all of the books would be of great help to him in teaching his classes. He ordered several volumes but expressed deep disappointment that it would take so long to have them delivered.

"Don't you have any you can sell me right now?" he asked.

From the bottom of his satchel Benson fished out several small tracts he kept on hand to give to interested prospects. But the only book he had was *The Marvel of Nations,* by Uriah Smith. This he gave to Gent. It was an inexpensive volume, but it served as a fair token of his gratitude for the hospitality he had received.

The two men talked on about varied beliefs they shared. The sun went down, and the crickets came out to chirrup loudly. They had become so friendly that Wendall decided to admit he was an Adventist. His approach was to ask a question: "Mr. Gent, do you know that Methodists are keeping the wrong day as the Sabbath?"

Gent bristled immediately, insisting that his church kept Sunday because Christ rose from the dead on that day, hence it must be right.

"Why," he demanded, "which do *you* believe is the right day to keep?"

"Get your Bible," Benson replied, "and let's see what our only real authority says."

Gent was led from text to text and was greatly distressed not to be able to find a single reference to support his belief that Sunday was the correct day of worship. The hour grew late—nine o'clock, ten o'clock. Finally, at eleven o'clock, Deacon Gent disconsolately bowed his head and admitted defeat. There was a moment of silence; then he stood up and offered his hand to Benson, knowing by now, of course, that Wendall was a Seventh-day Adventist.

"Young man! You've just got your church a convert! By the help of God I will keep the seventh day as the Sabbath from now on. I will not report for work tomorrow!"

Wendall Benson walked back to his room that night elated. He couldn't have been happier even had his briefcase carried orders from several dozen homes in Farmington.

In prayerful thanks to God for His divine guidance, he was not unmindful of the obviously providential way he had been spared from that boxer. Whatever happened to him, he wondered? He never learned.

As for Deacon Gent, when his fellow members in the

Methodist church learned he had succumbed to one of those wily "Seven-day Advents," they were at first aghast, then bitter, then defiant. Rough days were ahead. The fireworks began the very next Sunday when he was asked to teach a class and inevitably displayed his newly acquired knowledge, which he felt duty-bound to expound.

Colporteur Wendall Benson's one contact was to become an avalanche of untold importance. Only God knows the number of believers in the seventh-day Sabbath who were the result of his perseverance and devotion to what he felt to be his duty.

DETERMINATION

Although Deacon Gent was fully persuaded in his own mind that the seventh day was the true Sabbath, he had not decided what his relationship to the Methodist Church would be by the next day, Sunday. So perhaps it was more by force of habit than anything else that he took his place in his regular pew.

Sunday school superintendent Roger Worth, not knowing the marked change of heart and mind of this ordinarily mild-mannered member of his church, informed him that the teacher of the young men's class was ill that day. Would he fill the vacancy? The subject of the lesson was an easy one: the Ten Commandments.

For a moment—but only a moment—the deacon hesitated. The lesson was on the Ten Commandments! Was this simply a coincidence, or divine providence providing him with the opportunity to dispense his new-found light? Well, he would just have to wait and see how he would be led to deal with the subject. He nodded his head at Roger amiably, as he knew he was expected to—as he always did.

Opening his Bible to gather his thoughts, he found that he had left the ribbon marker at Exodus 20 where he had underlined in red the references to the seventh day. The red underlining seemed to pick up the ruby from the stained-glass windows beside him and glowed ethereally. The text staring up at him dared him to speak out. He was being given a providential opportunity, one voice seemed to say. Another voice reminded him that if he did, it would be heresy, pure and simple!

Gent still hadn't made up his mind when he stood before the group of twenty young men in the class that met in the basement of the church. Here they were well insulated from the rest of the classes when they became rowdy, as they frequently did. At the moment there was silence as he began to call the roll. All eyes were upon him. He squirmed uncomfortably under their close scrutiny. Did he hear what was being whispered about him? If he did, he gave no evidence of it.

"John Lewis Shuler," Gent intoned.

"Here," grinned John from his usual place on the front row, which he himself chose in his eagerness to learn all he could about his new faith. He sat next to two of the other boys who had taken their stand with him at Billy Sunday's that night. He had never seen Gent before, but Barney had. He leaned over and whispered, much too loudly, to John: "Boy! They sure picked a dilly of a substitute for Mizz Webster! This poor galoot is as loony as they make 'em!"

"Sh-h-h-h!" John cautioned Barney. "Not so loud!"

The lesson went well, Gent thought. He went quickly through all ten of the commandments, commenting as he ordinarily would have on each one. Then, feeling slightly giddy, he found himself taking the fatal step that was soon to separate him forever from the church he had learned to love since his youth. He cleared the nervous huskiness that threatened to choke him.

"Let's go back and look at the fourth commandment." He began reading, " 'Remember the sabbath, to keep it holy. Six days shalt thou labour, and do all thy work: but the seventh day is the sabbath of the Lord thy God.' " He paused. Which day *is* the seventh day of the week?"

Several voices called out at once, "Sunday."

"Are you sure?" Gent said, suddenly surging with confidence as his eyes fell upon a large lumber-company calendar hanging on the wall where all could see it. Heads pivoted silently, following him as he stepped to the calendar to put a bony finger on the column of Sundays.

"Which day of the week does Sunday fall on?" he asked quietly. There was not a sound in the room as the boys sat in puzzled wonderment.

"Surprised, aren't you? That was my first reaction last week when I had this fact pointed out to me by a Bible student. Up to then I'd never given a second thought about believing that Sunday—which is clearly the first day of the week—was not the true Sabbath, which is Saturday, the seventh day of the week." Gent counted out the days with his finger, letting it remain on the column of Saturdays in significant silence.

It took only a moment. Then there was bedlam. More than one of the older boys stoutly defended Sunday as the Sabbath because Jesus rose from the grave on that day.

"But what do we do with the fourth commandment, then?" the deacon asked quietly. "Do we accept all the others, and change this one to suit the dictates of our church and ignore the Bible, the Word of God?"

"Only Jews keep Saturday!" one bright boy jeered. "Are you trying to make Jews out of all of us?"

Loud laughter echoed derisively in the basement.

The deacon was adamant. When a semblance of order was restored, he merely held up his Bible to declare: "If any of you can show me one text where the Lord tells us to keep the first day, then I will continue to keep Sunday. But if you can't do it, then I can do nothing else but keep Saturday as the Sabbath, as the fourth commandment clearly demands."

As the bell rang for classes to close, Deacon Gent made one final appeal.

"I realize this has been a shock to you, as it was to me," he stated. "But if any of you would like to study further on the subject and look for texts that may give us help on Sunday observance, I'll be happy to have you come to my home this afternoon at three o'clock."

Superintendent Worth beamed at Gent as they shook hands after church.

"How'd it go with the boys this morning, Deacon? They must have enjoyed you," he said with a smile. "They were so quiet until closing time; then you must have told them a joke that set them to howling. We've never had that much laughter before from the nether regions!"

"Oh, I think they'll remember me, all right," Gent admitted modestly, "but I doubt if they or you will ever want me to take their class again."

And he left Roger Worth standing there wondering what he had meant by that last remark. He was soon to find out.

As it happened, only the three pals, John, Barney, and Bip, elected to go to the deacon's home that afternoon. It was just as well that none of the others went, because for some reason Gent began reading from the book of Revelation about some terrible beast with seven heads and ten horns. The boys tried to listen as long as they could, then made an excuse and told him they had to go.

Gent, realizing he had muffed his chance to interest the boys, handed John *The Marvel of Nations*, the book Benson had given him.

"Read this, boys," he said hopefully. "It'll explain the meaning of the dragon." As they walked home, John was the first to admit that Barney had been right.

"Gent's got some buttons missing somewhere," he said, trying his best to be kind in his judgment of the deacon. "I hope he doesn't get so bad they have to lock him up."

The other boys cared nothing for reading of any kind, so John kept the Uriah Smith book and began poring over it that very night in his room by the light of his kerosene lamp. He discovered that it dealt with the United States in prophecy—a subject he found intensely interesting.

When John finished the book, he returned it to the deacon and asked whether he had any others like it. It was then he learned that the book was one of many published by Seventh-day Adventists. Mr. Gent told him about Wendall Benson's visit, but it was evident that the colporteur never reached the Shuler home; at least John was never to meet that representative of the publishing house. But he did get the publisher's address in Battle Creek, Michigan, and wrote at once for further information—especially about the Sabbath question. In due time he received such a volume of mail that his parents became alarmed.

In the months that followed, John kept ordering books from the Adventist headquarters and studying them diligently, thoroughly comparing the ideas they presented with the Bible, thinking his way through each subject. His conclusion was that as far as he was concerned, there was no longer a Sabbath *question*. Saturday *was* the Sabbath! It was the only day God had ever blessed and asked man to keep holy.

In his enthusiasm, John took his Bible and other reading material to his parents and brothers and sisters, but they were not about to be convinced. The only matter they were convinced of was that he had gone off the deep end and was in over his head in this "foolish nonsense."

His mother grew grave and silent. Her large brown eyes were often misty as she looked wistfully at her son during mealtimes. She had never expected that her wish that he would take an interest in religion would culminate in his total absorption in something so foreign to her way of thinking.

His father took a stronger, more positive stand.

"Don't go any further into this seventh-day foolishness!" he commanded. "These Advents have given you crazy ideas. You go one step more and we'll be having you committed to the asylum over at Bartonville!"

John had a sudden flashback to what he had thought about Mr. Gent. Maybe the deacon hadn't had a few screws loose after all. In reality he and Gent had more in common than he had realized!

Father Shuler, having put his foot down, further prohibited John from reading the Bible, and promised to burn any of "that silly Advent" reading material he found lying around. Furthermore, he admitted to his wife his stern decision that if John kept on with this "seventh-day foolishness," he was going to put him out of the house and wouldn't let him continue living under the same roof with them.

When Mother Shuler confided to her son what his father had decreed, John was shocked. He had no idea where he would go if he were expelled from home. Nevertheless, he had no intention of giving up his faith. John's square jaw was certainly no sign of weakness. He carefully collected all his tracts, books, and Bible and took them to a secret hiding place where he could spend his spare time in reading them.

On one important point John, for the present, relented. He thought it unwise to press his stand on Saturday as the Sabbath, and continued to accompany his father to the mine on Saturdays. Whether that was consistent with what he believed with all his heart was right was not considered then. The immediate result was that his concession so pleased his father that when he asked his permission to talk to the men about religion during their lunch hour, he condescended—however reluctantly. Undoubtedly he reasoned that his son would soon make a fool of himself with his stuttering and the "craziness" of this whole Bible business.

John was never to forget that first day when he began his sermonizing to the miners. He ate his lunch before noon as he turned the crank sending his drill into the coal vein. When the noon whistle blew, he picked up an empty blasting powder can and took it with him to the shaft where the men ate their lunch. Then, using the bottom of the upturned can as his pulpit, he began talking about his new religious experience. There was insufficient light to read his Bible, but by now he had already committed many texts to memory—a habit he was to follow the rest of his life.

The miners—perhaps more out of respect for John's being the son of their union president than anything else—listened quietly without comment. What surprised them most—John's father most of all—was that the boy stuttered hardly at all. True, he spoke slowly and carefully, thinking his way through each sentence as he told them of his new, more meaningful way of life with faith in the hereafter since Billy Sunday had come to town. He explained that his speaking to them was part of the covenant he had signed at his conversion, to share his faith.

John could see none of the ten men in his captive audience. Only flickering flames about an inch in diameter, shining feebly from the oil lamp on each man's cap, marked their shadowed faces. Faintly outlined in the light of his own lamp was the black tin container he knelt before as his speaker's podium, which measured a foot in diameter and was two feet high.

Under such conditions, he had no blushing to worry about, and no distracting motions from the men to break his chain of thought. So it was that from that day forward, as long as his father permitted him to do so, he spoke to the men, perfecting his delivery a little more as the weeks passed. It failed to disconcert him that there was never a single comment—pro or con—from any of his listeners. Or were they really listening? No doubt some of them, after finishing their lunch, spent the rest of the time napping. John never knew.

What he did discover, however, was that he began to enjoy giving his little sermonettes. Was it then that he started to wonder whether, like Billy Sunday, he might have a call to preach? Actually, they had something in common: neither had any education to speak of, which was not a real handicap because it permitted them to speak on the level of the common man. Was it wishful thinking for John to dream that perhaps he too might one day stand before thousands and call them to Christ?

But his notion was quickly squelched when it was forcefully brought to mind that he didn't even have the intestinal fortitude to stand up for what he believed to be the Sabbath. The more he dwelt on the subject, the more his conscience bothered him. And the auger, as he turned the crank to bore it into the coal, seemed to groan, "It's Sabbath! It's Sabbath!" John was miserable.

"What if 150 feet of slate, rock, and dirt should cave in on me while I'm working some Saturday?" he reproached himself aloud as he worked in the pit.

Some Saturdays the mine did not operate. What a relief that was! He knew beforehand which Saturdays he wouldn't have to work, because the company had a unique way of signaling the operation of the mine. At five o'clock in the afternoon on Friday, one blast of the whistle meant, "No work tomorrow"; three blasts meant, "Everybody works tomorrow." John was elated by one blast but cut to the heart when it sounded three times.

At last, however, he reached the point of no return. He could no longer salve his conscience. He told his mother that no matter what the cost, he could not work another Saturday, because it was the Sabbath. She grew extremely agitated at this unwelcome news and begged him not to approach his father about his decision.

"Oh, John Lewis!" she pleaded, "you know how opposed he is to this Saturday business. He may give you a terrible beating and tell you to leave home!"

John knew she was right; he also knew that *he* was right. How could he continue to do otherwise than obey God and keep the commandment he knew by heart? He left the house and walked for miles into the woods, wrestling with his conscience, praying earnestly that God would help him to meet this extremity in his life. The fourth commandment was but one of many texts he had memorized during his studies. There were also two texts from the Psalms that he repeated over and over in his time of trouble! "Call upon me in the day of trouble; I will deliver thee, and thou shalt glorify me," and "This poor man cried, and the Lord heard him, and saved him out of all his troubles" (Ps. 50:15; 34:6).

Then, suddenly, the weight on his heart was gone. He no longer felt any desire to belabor the Lord further. It just seemed that his prayers had been answered. He turned in his tracks and walked home, determined to face his father like the man he felt he had just become. This was on a Thursday night. He didn't care whether the Friday whistle blew three times or not. It didn't matter. He would not be there on Saturday. That was that! After supper, when mother was clearing the table, he spoke up. His voice was calm; he did not stutter. He stated simply, "Father, my conscience has been troubling me about working on Saturdays. May I have your permission to stop going to the mine on Saturdays?"

There was a long pause. Was this the buildup to an explosion? If so, John steeled himself.

He was almost, but somehow not quite, prepared for the reply he got. His father pushed his chair from the table and said quietly, "You may do as you please about it, John." The words clipped out his edict.

"Thank you, Father," John replied softly, as though he had expected the reply, and smiled broadly at his mother, who stood as though transfixed. He had counted on God's hearing his prayer. He had not been disappointed. God had softened his father's heart as He had softened the hardhearted Pharaoh's long ago.

9

ORDINATION

Pressure and belittling jibes about his strange faith continued to plague John for the next five years, both at home and whenever he contacted his former friends. Barney and Bip soon gave up all pretense of being Christians and accused John of making a martyr of himself by dropping out of the gang's beer busts and poker parties. However, John felt no remorse for his change of life style. In fact, he had never been happier in his life. There were new motives for living. Whether he would ever become a minister was beside the point.

John's moral preparation for the responsibility soon to be thrust upon him was commensurate with his physical growth, his mental development, his tenderness of heart. Developing as a Christian in a crude environment, subjected to the influences of roughness, intemperance, and immorality, he matured into a clean, wholesome young man, enjoying the favor of both men and women who shared his Christian faith. As often as he could, he shared in the sports and pleasures of his youthful contemporaries, yet at no point did he yield to those human weaknesses that impair the moral stamina, the physical powers, or his influences as a Christian.

As he continued to give his sermonettes to the miners, John began to sense his need of further education, and decided to take up where he had left off and enter the ninth grade in high school. His father immediately approved. In fact, seeing that John was cut from a mold obviously dissimilar from any of the others in the Shuler family and that he had determination and the capacity for a high caliber of self-discipline, John Lewis, Sr., held out a choice plum which he believed would serve as a real incentive to lure John away from his ministerial leanings.

"John," he began one night after supper, "I want to talk to you seriously about your future. As I've told you a number of times, you've got a good head on your shoulders. You're analytical, you're a good organizer, and most of the time you tend to think straight—except when you're thrown in with some of those 'new thinkers' who mix you up with their strange ideas of religion, like these crazy Advents!" he threw in caustically.

"They are Adventists, Father, not Advents," John objected. "They've taken the name *Adventist* because they believe in the soon coming of Christ to redeem this lost world. And if they have influenced me to follow their way of thinking and believing, it has not been because I've been mesmerized into it. I have studied the reasons for their teachings and have found out for myself how rational their beliefs are."

"Well, be that as it may," his father continued, "if you do well in high school, I'll pay your way through college and later send you to law school. With your hanging out your shingle—'John Lewis Shuler, Attorney at Law'—well, who knows, you might have the potential to become a Senator, Congressman, or even President Shuler! Wouldn't that sound fine!"

They both laughed. It was an unusual moment. They had never before shared such camaraderie. But it was not to last. John's face fell, realizing he could not share his father's enthusiasm.

"I do appreciate your offer, Father," he said soberly. "Being a lawyer would undoubtedly assure my future and bring me wealth. It would mean the opportunity to be someone of prominence and bring honor to the Shuler name. Yet knowing what I do now about the reasons God created us and our obligation to spread the gospel to this hopeless world, I must continue with my plans to become a minister."

John reached out to lay his hand on his father's. It was an unprecedented gesture; a tender attempt both to thank and to touch his father emotionally. But his father jerked his hand away in anger. His mouth curled in contempt. He spat out venomously, "A 'hopeless' world, is it? Well, let me tell you, the truth is, *you're* the one that's hopeless!"

There was an ominous pause. Then he pronounced his wrathful decision: "John Lewis, I won't turn you out of the house, as I should, but from this day on you are on your own. You'll pay for your room, board, and clothing—or provide them yourself. I'll see that you are employed nights at the mine so you can have your own income—though I don't see how you can study, go to school, and work too. But that's your problem!''

And it was a problem. John's strenuous program of attending classes during the day, working in the coalpits three or four nights a week from 6:00 P.M. to 11:00 P.M., and getting up at 5:00 A.M. to prepare his lessons for the day took every moment of his time and nearly every ounce of his energy. But despite the rigor of the program, he completed ninth grade with excellent commendation from his teachers. But even they chose law as the goal he should work toward.

When John started the tenth grade, the pressure of his program doubled. His subjects required more study, and the hours he could devote to his theological studies practically vanished. It was plain he would have to make a decision, one way or the other. Would he, or would he not, become a minister? If he was to be one, he would have to withdraw from high school—much as he realized a minister needed a general education and a degree to be looked up to and to succeed in his calling. The only alternative was to educate himself.

His decision to study for the ministry coincided with an unusual—or was it providential?—development in Farmington. In that small community of 1,500 inhabitants, which already struggled to support five churches, another was to be added, a Seventh-day Adventist. Whether the twenty-six founding members were the result of Wendall Benson's canvassing the town that summer, history does not reveal. It was certain, however, that Deacon Gent could be claimed as a convert by Benson, and indirectly, John Lewis Shuler also.

With the organization of the little Adventist congregation, a new church building was erected, and John, who gave his testimony at every opportunity, was more than once invited to take charge of the services on Sabbaths. This he did with such obvious enjoyment and enthusiasm that he soon overshadowed the leadership of Brother Gent—no longer Deacon, of course, as he had so long been known thereabouts.

The church members decided to elect John their local elder and sent his name to the Southern Illinois Conference, asking that an official be sent to perform the ordination ceremony. Elder P. G.

Stanley was sent for the momentous occasion and arrived one evening to take over the service. Every member of the little congregation was rounded up to make the event more meaningful.

Elder Stanley stood before them, a bit pompously, it seemed. "Will Brother John Lewis Shuler please come forward?" he asked.

John, seated near the front, stood up and walked to the podium, looking up into the startled eyes of the elder, whose white side whiskers seemed suddenly to flair conspicuously.

"Ahem!" he cleared his throat. "Are *you*, young man, the candidate the church has selected for ordination?" he asked incredulously.

"Yes, sir, I am," John Lewis smiled, his old habit of blushing for the slightest reason taking over after a long absence. The color slowly rose above his collar until his face was a deep pink.

"How old are you, son?"

"I'm 18, sir."

There was an awkward pause. Elder Stanley now appeared to be joining John in his embarrassment. He ran a finger around his collar, which had become too tight for comfort. He shook his head in disbelief at what was happening.

"Young man—er, Brother Shuler," he corrected himself. "Would you be kind enough to be seated for a moment? I think we ought to discuss this matter with the members of the church before we proceed."

John took his seat while the pastor carefully explained that he had been delegated to ordain an adult as elder for the Farmington church. He was almost certain that the denominational leaders would never condone his ordaining a mere boy.

"The title of elder implies a man of maturity," Elder Stanley stated kindly, speaking in a manner he usually reserved for a group of children. "I see," he continued, "that you have four mature men among you. Surely one of them would be more suitable as elder—if he is willing to serve. Would you four men be willing to have your names placed on a ballot and let the church decide which of you is to be elected to serve as elder?"

Gent and the three other older men stood up and nodded their heads in agreement.

"All right, brethren, thank you. If someone will prepare some slips of paper, we will ask each member to name his or her choice of local elder for the Farmington church. Write only one name on your slip and put it in the collection plate when I pass among you."

John believed he was not even being considered for the position, and his modesty forbade him from voting for himself, so he wrote Gent's name on his ballot.

When the votes were collected, Elder Stanley sat down at the Sabbath school table in front of the podium and began reciting the names aloud.

"John Shuler," he read, tossing a suspicious glance over his glasses at John, as though thinking he must have voted for himself. "John Shuler," he read from another slip. "John Shuler, John Shuler, John Shuler," he repeated again and again from each slip he opened. It looked like a frame-up. The elder opened the last slip, which was John's. "A. Gent!" the pastor announced in obvious disgust. Every vote had been cast for John, except his own for Gent.

Shaking his head in disbelief at this odd turn of events, plainly displaying his unwillingness and perplexity as to how to proceed, Elder Stanley at length stood up and called John to the front.

"Let us kneel, brother," he said meekly.

And, placing his hands on the boy's head as he had been delegated to do by the members of the Farmington church, he ordained John Lewis Shuler at 18 years of age to be, so far as we know, the youngest man ever officially appointed to serve as church elder of any Seventh-day Adventist church.

10

ELEVATION

It was an astonishing fact, and John found the reality of it difficult to assimilate. Here he was, an uneducated, untrained, country bumpkin who had been suddenly and inexplicably weeded from a gang of rough, unpolished youth—snatched from the inky darkness of a coalpit—and thrust into the spotlight of a church pulpit! As a mere youth of 18 years he had been given this grave responsibility and was being looked up to as shepherd of the new Seventh-day Adventist church of Farmington.

Of course it was true that there were only two dozen members in the church—with the addition of Brother Gent and himself. But it was also true that he was better qualified as a Bible student than Gent, or any of the other members, to be the church's pastor.

So it was that on this particular Sabbath morning he had arrived early to get ready for the services for which he was responsible. He sat alone in the quietness, breathing deeply of the redolent new pine pews, getting his thoughts together, planning his strategy, working out his own method of basic homiletics (of which he knew nothing) that he was to follow for the rest of his life. Almost from the moment he had been appointed local elder he had begun thinking about how he could enlarge the membership of his little church.

In his logical, legal-type thinking process, he reasoned that he must work up a series of subjects that would appeal to the average mind of his listeners—if there were to be any listeners. He couldn't help blushing at the thought of his failure to impress his fellow miners at their noon lunch meetings. They had not shown the slightest interest in anything he had said to them. Perhaps they had merely slept through his talks. The mere fact that no one had asked a single question or shown the slightest hint of rebellion against his taking up their lunchtime, which they usually spent chattering among themselves, was small comfort to this aspiring young evangelist.

Just how much Billy Sunday had inspired John in his manner of speaking or delivery of his messages is hard to say. It may have been slight because John saw and heard Billy Sunday only once. Yet the visual and mental impact must also have been powerfully effective, because John was never to forget the time he spent in Sunday's tent, and the appeal that led to his decision to become a Christian. Undoubtedly, many who had "hit the sawdust trail" that night had merely experienced a temporary emotional blitzkrieg. However, to John, the decision opened a thrilling, lasting, lifelong experience, because he had invited his Lord to become a part of his life. This had played no small part in the broadening and deepening of his dramatic personal transformation.

John felt that Sunday's strongest attraction had been his personal sincerity and the way he appealed to the reasoning power of his listeners, telling them frankly, "You don't have to understand all about Christianity before you accept it." He remembered the vivid mental pictures Sunday created that fastened truth like arrows into his hearers' hearts. This method was much more effective than using deep theological arguments.

If Sunday, with an education that continued no further than the ninth grade, had been able to surmount such an impediment in the career he had chosen, surely, John reasoned, there was hope for him, too.

He was not the athlete Billy was. However, he did not feel it appropriate for a religious leader to hop about the podium in a church. Perhaps it was all right for a former baseball star, but John Lewis was by nature more reserved, which was, after all, more fitting for a member of the clergy.

One Billy Sunday practice John adopted from his first appearance as a lay preacher in the pulpit of the Farmington church was to dress immaculately. He determined that although underneath he was still a sooty miner, he would never again look like one. He bought a new suit and dress shoes that effectively set him apart as a clean, well-dressed gentleman. With his fair complexion, dark-gray eyes, and luxuriant black hair neatly parted on the side, he was, to the eye of the beholder, a well-groomed, handsome young man of the cloth.

How was he to share his experience and faith with others, John wondered. To begin with, he worked out a plan by developing the subjects he wanted to preach about with a method that proved so simple and effective that he was to follow it throughout his active years of preaching, teaching, and writing.

First, he chose a topic he thought would whet the interest of his listeners, such as: "Heaven: where is it? How do we get there?" Next, he would look up the word *heaven* in his *Cruden's Concordance* and study every text dealing with the subject. Then, with the aid of the few Adventist books and tracts he had, he would enlarge on the topic and lead his hearers to a logical conclusion, helping them to accept his appeal and take a step closer in their relationship to God.

Among the many texts he had begun memorizing he found a number that were especially inspirational and invaluable guides. One, spoken by the prophet Jeremiah, seemed especially dear to the young man. "Call unto me, and I will answer thee, and shew thee *great and mighty things, which thou knowest not*" (Jer. 33:3).

This text guided him in his choice of subjects for his public meetings. He decided not to try to get the people of Farmington out to unpopular, scoffed-at Saturday services. Instead he got the word around that he was holding Sunday-night meetings at their new little church. How this was accomplished—whether through the local press or by handbills—John has forgotten. Nevertheless, whatever method he used, it served to spark interest—whether it was caused mostly by curiosity to see what the boy preacher had to say, or the strangeness of this "Saturday church cult." In any event, the pews of the little church were packed each Sunday—so long as John's topics held out!

Several years went by; then John was invited to attend an Adventist camp meeting held at Decatur, Illinois. This served not only to add to his meager store of books that inspired him to enlarge his ministerial repertoire but also to help him explore the depths of many topics as yet unknown to him, and to his Farmington flock.

The true importance of that camp meeting to John was not learned by him until a number of years later when he discovered that he had been spotted by a beautiful young woman who, from that time on, was never able to forget him.

As a strong, physically active young man, John had been asked to assist in various ways at the camp meeting. He readily agreed, but soon discovered that his coalpit pallor was a distinct handicap. The warm summer sun soon had his skin resembling a ripe tomato.

Someone suggested that lemon juice would not only ease John's tenderness but also help him attain a rich tan. So for a number of mornings before beginning his day's activities, he endured what must have been a stinging session behind his tent while he ran a cut lemon over his sunburned face, arms, and shoulders.

Whether or not this therapy had any beneficial effect on John, it had a profound effect on a beautiful young woman who was camping with her parents in the tent directly in front of his. She found John's ritual, which she watched each morning from behind a discreetly parted tent flap, most fascinating.

That young lady was Etta Rothrock, but John not only did not know her name, he didn't even know she existed. Neither did Etta learn John's name. But seeing him through her tent flap left an indelible impression. "Whenever I decide to get married," she told her mother, "that's just the type of young man I'm going to start looking for!"

11

RECOGNITION

For the next two years and three months—June, 1908, to September, 1910—John Lewis was to experience, roller-coaster fashion, times of deep discouragement and heights of elation. The "ups" included unexpected honorable recognition of his efforts as a lay preacher—being granted a ministerial license (which was next to being ordained as a full-fledged minister of the gospel) and being able to travel widely in Illinois as a denominational worker. The "downs" included being all but thrown out of a Methodist church where he had been invited to hold a series of meetings, and suffering unimaginable cold and all but starvation during the unusual situation in which he was placed while serving that Methodist community.

The peak of his roller-coaster experience—from which he was never to come down—was his eventually meeting the beautiful blonde who had seen him as the man of her dreams six years before. To admit John was in full agreement with her choice was to put it mildly. From the moment their eyes first met they were drawn to each other as though by magnets. Perhaps it was a reaction to the depths of his unhappy experiences prior to their meeting that helped create in him the ethereal altitude of emotions he and Etta May were to share.

John's first step up the success ladder came as a total surprise. The Sunday-night meetings he had held at his Farmington church had been a letdown; only one little old lady was baptized. Nevertheless, the brethren of the Southern Illinois Conference had their eyes on this "most unlikely worker." They were not unmindful of the tremendous effort he had been putting forth in that little hard-nosed town.

Conference president S. E. Wight had received nothing but good reports of John Lewis, whom he had been at first led to believe might turn out to be an unmanageable punk upstart. But suddenly the young man found himself basking in the warm sunshine of his superiors' smiles. Elder Wight wrote, inviting John to come to Stewardson, Illinois, first to help pitch tents for the camp meeting coming up in July, but later to join another young man a little older than himself in conducting a crusade with a tent of their own in a city where there were no Adventists.

However flattering the offer, John realized he wasn't ready for this sudden thrust into the limelight. In his reply he thanked the president profusely for the kind offer but suggested he was too young for such work and explained his educational limitations. Not only had he not completed tenth grade, but he had never received any formal denominational education. He simply did not consider himself qualified to preach—not yet, anyway. Perhaps his time would come, if it were God's will, he replied modestly.

Elder Wight was duly impressed, so impressed that a year later he felt it was now God's will for John to reconsider a more active role in His work. He repeated his invitation. This time it was to aid in setting up the camp meeting in Centralia, Illinois, then to join young Evangelist Elwood Ferris in conducting a tent crusade in Flora, Illinois.

Meanwhile, John had been spending every available hour in his self-directed program of ministerial training. The Bible remained his favorite and most-often-consulted source of instruction. He explored it for hours at a time. His memory became saturated with its language, his soul with its spirit, his life with its teachings. So familiar did he become with Scripture phraseology, so imbued with the Inspired Word's grand strain of thought and feeling, that he could scarcely express himself even in mundane affairs without some reference to Holy Writ. He now felt he was at least somewhat ready to embark on the Lord's work, so he accepted the call, cut the slender ties that remained between himself and his family, and took the train to Centralia.

At a conference session in connection with the camp meeting, the delegates voted, on August 15, 1909, to give John Lewis a ministerial license. John was elated. It was as though they had suddenly presented him with a gift of $5,000. It was not until several weeks later, after he and young Ferris had begun taking turns preaching in their own tent in Flora, Illinois, that he received official word from the conference committee that his wage had been set at five dollars a week!

John's wage at the mine had not been high, but neither had it been low for what was the prevailing wage at the time. He had generally averaged between four and five dollars a day. Now he had been granted the princely stipend of five dollars *a week!* Strangely enough, the incongruity of the fact was accepted with a shrug of his shoulders. Who was he to question the decision of his superiors—the Lord's workers? If God expected him to live on such a pittance, He'd provide a way. He simply replied in a letter to the conference treasurer: "Dear Sir: It will save both your office and my time and effort if before you send me my monthly check you deduct the tithe on my wages and send me the balance. Thank you for taking care of this matter for me. Sincerely, your brother, J. L. Shuler.

The young evangelist was soon to have the poverty of his church thrown in his face in an unexpected manner. One of the residents of Flora who attended their nightly meetings was pastor of the big Presbyterian church in town. When Shuler's partner, Ferris, was invited to give the Sunday-morning invocation at the Presbyterian church, he was astonished to hear the minister announce after his prayer: "This young man and his associate are preaching at the tent downtown. They are presenting some things contrary to Presbyterian doctrine. One of these teachings is that Sunday is not the Sabbath, according to the Bible—that Saturday is the true Sabbath. I must admit that I agree with them on this!"

When Elwood told John what had happened, they thought, Praise the Lord! What a big fish we've caught in the Lord's net! And John hurried down to visit the pastor in his plush, walnut-paneled study. Seated in a deep, leather-upholstered lounge chair, he looked around him with obvious satisfaction and exclaimed, "Oh, Doctor, we can't begin to tell you how happy we are that you have accepted the Sabbath! You will be a powerful influence for good in helping to spread the truths we have to offer your people!"

"Tut, tut, young fellow," the distinguished LL.D. replied, squinting through the bright rays of the morning sun. "Of course, I can't do that! It would mean giving up this fine parsonage and my salary of $500 a month—and my wife would probably leave me!"

John was stunned. Here was a modern example of Jesus' experience with the rich young ruler—a man who knew what was right but wasn't willing to pay the price. He was sacrificing his soul's salvation for the pleasures and comforts of the present that would mean nothing when it came time to meet his Maker. How would he then justify his decision? It was a stiff price to pay, John thought, even though his salary was twenty-five times what John received.

Summer passed. It grew too cold to sleep in the tent until the close of the campaign. How could John afford to rent a room, eat even simply, and have anything left for his bare necessities? It certainly seemed an impossible position to be in. Resigned as he might be to rent the most Spartan room, he couldn't afford even the cheapest one. Yet, somehow, he felt the Lord could provide for his needs if he was truly in His service. Elwood Ferris and his wife had no room to put him up, but they did provide his meals for $3 a week. Early on that crisp October afternoon, John tied the strings on the cold canvas flap of his tent and walked downtown. Before he had left he had told the Lord all about his problem and simply asked His guidance now in meeting his need. The wind was blowing up a gale that chilled him to the marrow. He tried to wrap his old woolen overcoat more closely around him, but it was too thin to be of much warmth.

How would it be possible to find a room? At the very least he would have to pay five or ten dollars a week. And even at that price the place might be hardly livable. He thought of the comfortable warmth of the old room he had enjoyed for so long under his parents' roof. Had he made a wise decision to leave dear old sooty Farmington after all? With the financial aid of his father, he could now be well on his way to becoming a wealthy lawyer rather than being thrust into the streets of a cold, disinterested city as a poor, impoverished preacher. Actually, he felt he was on a par with a beggar at this moment.

John's moment of anguish and doubt was short-lived. He was passing a huge two-story mansion only a few blocks from the tent. Wouldn't it be great to live nearby in such style and obvious comfort? But this was decidedly not a rooming house. Still, unaccountably, his footsteps seemed inclined to take him up to that massive front door with its impressive stained-glass ornamentation. He felt foolish ringing the bell. But what did he have to lose? Maybe someone would take pity on a poor beggar.

A fine-appearing middle-aged woman answered the door. John had almost expected a maid. He almost slipped back into his old habit of stuttering as he asked as cheerfully as he dared, "Pardon me, madam, b-but do you happen to have a r—room to rent?"

Perhaps his appearance went to the lady's heart. Maybe she thought he was stammering with the cold and felt sorry for him. In any case, in a moment he had been invited in and had stated simply that he was one of the evangelists holding meetings down the street and was looking for a place to stay for a few weeks until their campaign was over.

"Well, this is most odd!" she exclaimed, cocking her head almost parrotwise, her stylish bouffant hairdo reminding John of a Farmington friend's white-crested cockatoo.

"I have never thought of renting any of the rooms," she said, "but I simply can't imagine anyone living in a tent this time of year. Perhaps I might let you have one of my guest rooms—but only for a short time, you understand. Do you wish to see it?"

"Oh, yes indeed! Thank you so much, Mrs.——" John began, breaking off until she had introduced herself as Mrs. Thompson, the wife of a prosperous hardware store owner in the town.

The room John was shown was unbelievably sumptuous, with rich velvet maroon drapes, Oriental carpeting, and a high, canopied, feather bed. His heart sank. He knew he would never be able to afford anything like this. But when Mrs. Thompson said that if it suited him he could have it for just enough to "cover the cost of the steam heat and laundering the linens—a dollar and a half a week," he was aghast. He had to sit down for a moment, fanning himself in the luxury of the rush of the warmth from the radiator beside the bed.

He could hardly wait to get back to the Ferrises' little apartment to tell them how miraculously God had led him that afternoon. Here he was to be cared for like a king on a total of only four and a half dollars a week for room and board!

12

MATRIMONY

Young Evangelist John Shuler was unprepared for the letdown that came after the Flora campaign closed. He had been so spoiled by the luxury he had enjoyed in the Thompson mansion that he actually dreaded his next assignment, which began the following January and would run over into February, 1910.

It was an uncomfortable situation at best, right from the start. A tiny Baptist community eight miles out in the country near Martinsville, Illinois, had unaccountably requested that an Adventist minister be sent to them as a guest speaker. They agreed that it would be fine with them if the Adventist stayed on and conducted one of his revival campaigns they'd heard about.

The immediate problem was that there were no other Adventists within miles of the little village, and John would have to take potluck on where he'd stay each night—dependent upon the generosity of someone—anyone—in his audience.

That first night his hopes were high. The building was packed. And despite the fact that it was only 10° F. (which it remained during his entire stay), there was a big stove at each end of the room kept at almost white-hot heat by the janitor. In fact, it became so warm that John found himself sweating profusely right up to the time to go home in one of the members' buggies. That was like stepping from a steam bath into an icehouse.

How he managed to keep from freezing to death until he reached the home of his last-minute host, he could never understand. Usually it was two miles or more over the ice-crusted country lanes to the house where he was to stay, and even then he found, more often than not, that the family was so poor that there were often broken windowpanes in the ill-heated room he was given. More than once he awakened in the early morning, his teeth chattering, to find his blanket covered with snow that had sifted through the cracks—reminding him unhappily of some of his mother's mouth-watering pastries dusted with powdered sugar.

Breakfasts in the mornings, no matter how cheerfully served, were simply an impossibility! They included coffee, like mud, which he couldn't drink; the usual bacon, which he had to pass up; and grits with a big piece of pork fat that he had to fish out if he was to try to eat the mush at all. He managed to abide the heavy soda biscuits, which were far from being anything like his dear mother's fluffy, golden-brown ones. But he gulped them down as a last resort with the aid of generous helpings of sorghum molasses.

Poor John tried to take comfort in whatever passages of Scripture he could locate that might apply to his sad situation. The best he could find to fit was 2 Timothy 2:3, which besought him to "endure hardness, as a good soldier of Jesus Christ."

He did his best to present his sermons on the Second Coming, the signs of the times, the millennium, the home of the saved, and the prophecies of Daniel. The meetinghouse was continually packed. However, when he began dealing with Daniel 7:25, "And he shall . . . think to change times and laws," applying its meaning as shown by other scriptures, the bottom fell out of his crusade.

Despite the two red-hot stoves in the building, most of his Baptist audience seemed to freeze up solid on him that evening. The trustees met the next day and served notice that the building was closed to him for any further meetings. He was invited to leave the community. With no other building available, it was impossible for him to meet with those who were still interested. He could only send the conference an account of what had happened, and then follow instructions to go back to Martinsville, where arrangements would be worked out for him to conduct a crusade in the Adventist church.

It was from this moment that the picture was to glow with rosy unreality for John Lewis. It began with his being entertained as a guest in the fine home of Charles J. Rothrock who—was it by some strange coincidence?—happened to be the brother of Etta May, who still remembered John and who was living with her parents in Lakeland, Florida.

Unaccountably (that feeble word seemed to keep cropping up

in the life of John Shuler), Mr. and Mrs. Rothrock brought out the
family album, which, Charles was pleased to point out, contained
pictures of his pretty sister who was coming to visit them within a
few weeks. He wasn't slow about suggesting outright that John
and Etta would make a handsome couple. John blushed slightly,
smiled shyly, but didn't disagree. She was undoubtedly as pretty a
young woman as he had ever seen, and he began at once to look
forward to their meeting.

If it hadn't been for John's fortunate stay at the Thompson
place, where some of the elegance of Mrs. Thompson's manner of
living had rubbed off on him, he might have felt out of place at the
Rothrocks. Charles and his wife were comfortably well off, as were
Etta May's parents. They were used to the better things of life,
many of which John had not had in that little country mining town,
even though his father could have afforded some of them if he had
wanted to.

For instance, John was unacquainted with real oil paintings,
and was enthralled by the one he found in his room at the
Rothrocks. It pictured a thundering surf bursting over a rock, with
sea birds soaring gracefully across a storm-clouded sky. The
beauty of it drew him irresistibly. Yet when he examined it closely,
the impression faded, and it seemed merely careless daubings of
pigment. It was only when he stepped away from it that everything
came back into focus. Was there some trick to it? He wondered.
The pictures he had been used to at home were lithographs of
well-known works of art, but the prints were always sharp,
whether you looked at them from near or from across the room.

The Rothrocks also had a sizable library in their parlor, which
left him feeling uneducated and immature. There were so many
handsome volumes. How could any one family own and read so
many books of their very own? he puzzled. He caressed the
volumes affectionately, noting the titles of interesting histories to
which he felt a real kinship as a result of knowing their relationship
to many a Bible prophecy. He determined to read the best of them
as long as he had the opportunity.

The day came when Etta May arrived, and he was introduced.

"Etta May," Charles's voice was saying, "this is Mr. John
Shuler, the evangelist who has been staying with us." Whatever

else was said, John could never remember. He was lost in the vision of this pale, ethereal creature with wide, spiritual blue eyes and a wealth of golden hair. Her dress—whatever it was she wore—was as wonderful as she. She seemed a delicate flower on a slender stem. Her hand came out to his as she looked straight into his eyes.

There was no instant recognition on Etta's part. It was not until later, when she and John had the opportunity to be alone sitting together on the porch swing, that she had the strange experience of merging his image with that of the tomato-red face of the young man she had seen six years before at the Decatur, Illinois, camp meeting. It was then, as they compared notes on where they both had been at the time, that she was certain John was the one and the same—the man of her dreams!

Almost immediately John became aware of several frustrating facts: Not only was Etta May just short of finishing her degree as a registered nurse at the Orlando, Florida, Sanitarium, which put her miles above him educationally, but she was also being pursued by a large number of eligible suitors. Particularly, she was being urged by her mother to say Yes to a wealthy orange grower in Florida, George Manwell. Another of her wooers was an Adventist minister, as successful as he was handsome, who lived not far from her home in Lakeland, Florida. Was this angelic vision to become a reality for him, or was she to vanish into someone else's arms? John agonized.

Despite the fact that they had immediately hit it off, John was fearful of losing her while he was conducting a tent campaign in the little town of St. Elmo. When that duty ended, he was promptly sent to aid in the camp meeting at Shelbyville, Illinois, being held from August 8 to 18, 1910. It was there that the plot thickened, for Charles Rothrock and his wife turned up to attend the meetings and were accompanied by Etta May, who had decided not to return to Lakeland but to stay longer at her brother's.

John and Etta's courtship blossomed. They couldn't bear to be out of each other's sight. They determined not to wait until an elaborate wedding could be planned. The date was set for September 18, a month after camp meeting closed. At that time the tents were still up.

Etta and John exchanged vows in the twelve-by-fourteen-foot tent in which her brother, his wife, and their son, Kenneth, had lived during the encampment and had remained until the wedding. The ceremony was performed by Elder E. A. Bristol, who had succeeded Elder Wight as president of the conference. Someone noticed that in their haste to tie the knot, the bride had not been provided with even a bouquet. At the last minute a double fistful of dandelions growing about the tent was handed to Etta.

The newlyweds were greeted by the few friends and family present, then John pulled a five-dollar bill from his pocket and handed it to Elder Bristol. The elder quickly handed it back, remarking wryly, "You keep it, John; you need it a lot more than I do!"

No truer words were ever spoken. That five-dollar bill was the only money John had to his name. He later learned that Etta had fifteen dollars in her purse. Between them they had twenty dollars, the clothes they wore, and what they had in their suitcases.

It seemed a poor start for their years ahead, but Etta and John determined from the beginning that they would rely on God to look after their needs. Although Etta's parents were well able to set them up in housekeeping comfort, she requested no help from them. John had told her of his remarkable experience in being guided to the Thompson mansion when he needed housing so badly. Perhaps, he said wistfully, the good Lord would provide for them now as He had then. They wouldn't even mind if it wasn't so lavish. But such was not to be their fortune—at least not at first.

They laughed until their tears flowed when the first "answer" to their prayers came with the announcement that John's salary as a married man had been raised from five dollars a week to seven! Despite the disappointing fact that they were expected to live on six dollars and thirty cents a week after their tithe had been deducted, they resolved not to go into debt. And somehow, by the blessing of God, they managed to get by.

Etta never once complained about their hard lot, but readily adjusted to the immediate situation of living in a twelve-by-fourteen-foot tent, with only a bed, a little gasoline stove for cooking, a stack of boxes for a cupboard, a few dishes and pots, and a wooden box for a dining table. There was no time for a honeymoon. John's work began immediately.

There were days both bright and dark ahead of them in the more than sixty-one years they were to spend together, but they were never to regret their marriage. From that day Etta supported John 100 percent in all his plans to win souls for the Master.

13

ADVERSITY

Although 1913, which found John and Etta in Jacksonville, Florida, had an auspicious beginning for the promising young couple, it also held in store some of the most traumatic days they were ever to experience.

Of most importance was the fact that Etta was expecting her firstborn in the latter part of the summer, and all their plans centered upon that happy event. After all, wasn't this a time most appropriate for happiness?

The Shulers were content in the cozy little apartment they had rented. True, it was not situated in the best part of town, but false pride was never to be one of their besetting sins. They were able to laugh often at the memory of how they had set up housekeeping in their "honeymoon cottage" with only boxes for furniture in a camp meeting tent. Their life was now decidedly more comfortable, but of course still not up to the standards Etta had been used to all her life.

John recalls how in those early days of his ministry he and Etta often had to sit down and figure ever so carefully what to do to make their funds stretch far enough to cover bare necessities. That was when a dollar was worth a hundred cents, and prices had not begun to soar into the economic stratosphere. The average apartment rental within their price range was between twenty and twenty-five dollars a month, and a good loaf of wheat bread cost seven cents. A half-gallon of milk with lots of rich cream on top was only fifteen cents, and gasoline could often be found at ten cents a gallon.

John's best black suit had cost only twenty-five dollars; his shoes, six. Etta still had a lot of good-quality clothes left from her college days; therefore, expense for her wardrobe was at first minimal. She expected to purchase a few plain maternity dresses as she approached her sixth month of pregnancy; otherwise, there were no extra expenditures in the offing. It was well that there were none, because they had been able to save nothing so far on John's minimal stipend—it hardly could be called a salary by any standard, even in those days.

All young evangelists and ministers were used to following literally, not by choice, but by necessity, the Biblical example of God's first messengers, who had "neither purse, nor scrip." This was because of the scarcity of funds available to the growing Adventist Church, with, at the same time, endless demands from the worldwide field. When John had to make infrequent out-of-town speaking engagements, he traveled by train, sat in the second-class coach, and never indulged in patronizing the dining car. Instead, he took along some fruit, nuts, raisins, and other snacks that would allay his hunger until he got to his destination.

Living in God's glorious sunshine rather than in the murky gloom of a coal mine was one of John's greatest consolations for which he was constantly grateful. His happiness was now settled on a few basic factors: he was living simply, devoid of any thought of self-seeking, while training himself to think clearly and accurately, and he was storing his mind with useful thoughts. His motives in dedicating his life to bringing the gospel to his fellow men left no room for self-centeredness, and the close fellowship he experienced day by day with the Master brought him enduring satisfaction and the peaceful knowledge that he was under divine protection and constant guidance every hour.

John and Etta were not at all worried about the way their life would be affected by the arrival of their child. They accepted it as a fact that rearing an infant would enrich their lives, and were certain that God would help them plan their future to compensate for the added responsibility. Healthwise, Etta was unconcerned about carrying her child. She had always enjoyed the best of health, and there were no complications to worry her as she began her seventh month.

Although John longed to attend the forthcoming General Conference session and meet with church members from around the globe, he did not qualify as a delegate, and he had no money to make the trip to Takoma Park, Maryland. But the members of the

Jacksonville church, which he pastored (it was the only regular pastorate he was to hold during his long years of service), knew he wanted to attend, so they passed the hat and raised enough money to send the young couple. Immediately Etta began packing their bags for the expected train trip. Then John got a bright idea.

Living as they were only about a dozen miles from the Atlantic, oceangoing liners and freighters regularly steamed up the deep channel of the St. John's River to dock in the heart of downtown Jacksonville. John had heard of a freighter that ran regularly between Jacksonville and Baltimore and took on a few passengers each trip. When he inquired about the fare, he was surprised to learn that he and Etta could book passage that included both berth and meals for less than fare alone on the train.

Etta shared his enthusiasm for this new adventure and looked forward to making the trip. The voyage northward, following the coast and up the Chesapeake Bay, proved most pleasant but otherwise uneventful. They took the train from Baltimore to Washington, and were soon in Takoma Park. The sessions were inspiring. Special emphasis was placed upon the growing importance of evangelism in all parts of the world, an emphasis with which John was in hearty agreement. Plans laid for the furtherance of evangelistic endeavors throughout the United States indicated a rising sun of opportunity and promise for young evangelists such as John Lewis Shuler.

Despite the note of optimism and halo of happiness with which the Shulers left Washington, their return trip on the steamer was destined to shape the future of John and Etta more than anything that transpired at the conference.

Aboard the vessel, they felt more relaxed with the conclusion of the business sessions behind them. They spent hours on deck after settling in their cabin, seeing ships from almost every port in the world coming and going in the busy harbor. But an hour or two after they were underway, they began to experience the first strong surges of the open water. That was when Etta began having misgivings about the wisdom of having taken the steamer, knowing that there was no doctor aboard. What if she ran into difficulties with either seasickness or her pregnancy?

John, covering up his own apprehension, tried to reassure her.

"I once heard an old sailor say that to keep from getting seasick all you have to do is keep your eyes on the horizon and never look down at the sea," he said, speaking with more assurance than he felt.

"But what if you can't see the horizon?" Etta hiccupped, peering into the thick fog bank that had suddenly engulfed the ship.

"Let's go below and ask the steward," John quipped weakly, attempting to smile, but his own coloring was beginning to show a yellowish tinge. With considerable difficulty they managed to reach their cabin and throw themselves on their bunks. "If we hadn't eaten lunch, perhaps we wouldn't be so nauseated," John groaned.

But Etta, more alarmed than he, managed to ring the bell for the stewardess. An eternity seemed to pass before a disheveled head appeared at the door. For a moment the woman took in the situation with glassy eyes; then, without even attempting to ask a question, she lurched out the door, managing to declare over her shoulder in a quavering voice, "My dear, I can't do a thing for you! I'm d-d-deathly sick myself!"

Within an hour John and Etta realized that the worst was happening. Etta's nausea was bringing on a miscarriage. What could they do? Poor John struggled up to the captain's quarters and told him what was happening to his wife.

The captain immediately ordered the telegrapher to send out an SOS, explaining the situation and asking whether any ship nearby could send a doctor to them. John sat helplessly by while the wireless operator continued tapping out the message. The telegrapher explained that his ship, being small, did not have as efficient sending equipment as did the company's larger vessels. He only hoped his messages would be strong enough and reach far enough to bring help.

"Even if my signal gets to another of our ships, which should be passing about now, there's only about one chance in ten that there will be a doctor aboard," the operator stated matter-of-factly.

"But I'll keep trying, Reverend!" he promised as John returned to his cabin to check on Etta's progress.

Neither crew members nor passengers were in sight. Outside,

the night moaned and sobbed to the accompaniment of shrieking air. Tremendous dull blows made the ship tremble as she rolled under the weight of the towering waves toppling on her deck.

Etta's groans of pain reached John down the passageway before he was even near their cabin door.

"Oh, dear God! Help me! *Help me!*" she moaned plaintively.

Tears streamed down Etta's face as she told John that the baby was being born. Had the Lord deserted them in their extremity? They both prayed, pouring out their hearts in their pleading, John bowing on the cabin floor beside Etta.

John explained to Etta the efforts that were being made to contact another ship and find a doctor, and encouraged her to have faith. He tried to console her as well as himself with passages he had memorized from the Psalms. " 'Call upon me in the day of trouble: I will deliver thee, and thou shalt glorify me,' " he quoted.

There was a rap at their cabin door. A crewman had been sent with the good news that a sister ship, passing on her way from Jacksonville to Baltimore, had heard their message. And, wonder of wonders, there was an obstetrician aboard who would try to reach them!

There were, however, several serious problems about rendez-vousing with the other ship: it was night, and their meeting place was off treacherous Cape Hatteras where for centuries countless ships had foundered on the ragged shoals. It still devoured a number of ships each year. The other vessel had a deeper draft than theirs so it had to keep farther out to sea. On the other hand, the smaller ship had to remain closer to shore because of the mountainous seas. One thing was in their favor: the fog had lifted, so the ships were able to approach within a quarter mile of each other. It took nearly two hours to rendezvous. Meanwhile, the doctor sent word that he was traveling without his instruments and instructed the cook to boil a number of long-handled kitchen spoons that he could use as forceps.

The wind eased a little, but the sea ran as high as ever. Passengers and crew on both ships who had learned of the dramatic rescue under way braved the cold to line the railings of both ships and watch as the vessels came as close as they dared. Then, under their searchlights, a lifeboat was launched, and a rope ladder let down from the big ship. All watched breathlessly as the doctor and two seamen climbed down the ladder and managed to get into the wildly bobbing boat.

After a battle to cross the plunging waves between the ships, the doctor and crew finally scrambled aboard the smaller vessel. Within minutes the obstetrician had delivered the Shuler baby, done what he could to ease Etta's pain, and was on his way back to the big vessel standing by.

The baby, a boy, had been born dead. Grief-stricken, John and Etta looked at the perfectly formed infant, then, numbed and speechless, at each other. Why had they been brought through this ordeal? They had been so providentially helped, yet their child had been taken from them. Silently, John placed the doll-like body in a shoebox and took it to the ship's stern. There, with tears mingling with the salty spray, he committed it to the angry sea. A giant wave swallowed it in one crashing gulp of instant obliteration.

Shortly after the ships parted, the captain came to John and asked for his opinion.

"Reverend," he began, making use of the customary term of respect for men of the cloth to which John objected strenuously, "you will need to make a decision. If you think your wife should be hospitalized, we will change our course and make harbor at Charleston, South Carolina. However, if you wish to take full responsibility for your wife's care in her cabin, we'll go on to Jacksonville."

John talked it over with Etta, and because she was much improved physically, they decided it would be wise to get back to Jacksonville as quickly as possible. Once they docked there, it would be only a short trip by taxi to their apartment. Then Etta could be attended by her own doctor.

With this decision made, and the rough weather clearing considerably, they felt more comfortable. This left their remaining hours aboard the steamer free for the deep introspection and soul searching their ordeal demanded.

How could they account for this tragic loss of their first child? Would God grant them another to take its place? Why had not the child been allowed to live, seeing it had matured so perfectly during its seven-month gestation?

John's eyes clouded with tears when he allowed himself to dwell upon that indelible memory of his own flesh and blood lying so still in death, yet so perfect in detail: those tiny fingers and hands, the feet and toes, and that beautifully shaped head with its angelically innocent face! Could there be any logical reason for the loss of the infant, especially after being so miraculously delivered at sea in answer to their prayers? How could God expect them to look up through their soul-rending tears of sorrow and murmur, " 'Thy will be done' "?

In an agony of frustration John searched his Bible for an answer—any answer or consolation he could find. Was there a solution in Job's experience? Job suffered far more than John and Etta had, with the loss of all his children, his health, and his wealth. God had allowed Satan to interfere in Job's life for a reason. There must also be a reason for his and Etta's tribulation. If only he could differentiate between what God causes and what God allows!

Had he been wrong in arbitrarily getting tickets for steamer travel without seeking God's guidance before making that decision? Still, it was within God's power to have overruled and saved them from this peril, he reasoned. He sought solace in the Beatitudes but was bewildered by the words "Blessed are they that mourn." How was this possible?

Yet it was this text—so inexplicable at first—that began to open John and Etta's understanding to the stern lessons that could be drawn from their experience. They were both certain that John had been called to the ministry, but had their prayers for a child been God's will. Wasn't it possible that His plans for them would be too strenuous and time-demanding for establishing a permanent home? Had this been a form of divine discipline, similar to that possibility suggested by one of Job's friends to the prophet?

It was part of God's intention, John reasoned, that Job's troubles would culminate in greater spiritual insight, lasting peace, and greater blessing for him than he had ever dreamed possible. However, it was Satan's plan to weaken Job's will and destroy his dependence and commitment to God. This thought was somewhat consoling to John. Still, it was hard to reconcile himself to that other familiar but troublesome text, "All things work together for good to them that love God."

How, Jonn and Etta asked themselves, could this experience help them to develop greater strength of character? Had their child been taken to help them understand that being Christians was no insurance policy against suffering? They agreed that this was a conceivable possibility.

John—ever the practical lawyer in his thinking—took all the reasons for their loss he could think of, and presented them to his mental jury. Had he as a young, inexperienced minister been brought through this fiery furnace of soul torture to prepare him better to enter into the feelings of his fellow men, to learn that sympathy is so much more related to sorrow than it is to joy? He had already seen ministers of many denominations who were so insulated from real life that their fountain of sympathy had run dry. They met the troubles of their parishioners with unfeeling, unseeing eyes. Meeting them was like being confronted with the cold gaze of a marble statue.

With the tragic experience behind him, John realized that he could at least better understand and sympathize with those whom he would be called upon to serve. It helped him to see new meaning in the text that admonished him to "rejoice with them that do rejoice, and weep with them that weep." And he and Etta now knew a little of what it meant to God to lose His own Son in death. His death had been temporary. They believed that their little one would also be returned to their arms if they remained Christians.

The trial of their faith had helped them reach a higher plateau of Christian character. They became reconciled to the knowledge that they were not to have children, that their lives were to be devoted entirely to God's work. Undoubtedly their conclusion was divinely inspired, for although Etta's physician was later to pronounce her in perfect health, she never bore another child.

14

EVANGELISM

As an unconverted youth, John Lewis had not been even an average reader. During the time he was getting his formal education, he was anything but a bookworm.

His becoming a Christian furnished the motivation for numerous habit changes. With his new experience came an insatiable thirst for knowledge—especially for basic facts that would prove to his own mind he had been right in his decision to follow the teachings of Christ. The first alarming evidence his family had that "Buck" had vanished was when the new John Lewis started carting armloads of reading material up to his room, where, like a 150-pound sponge, he began soaking up the information he needed to round out his new life.

In the Adventist publications he requested were frequent references to a writer by the name of Ellen G. White, whom he began to recognize as a woman of great mentality. Not only did she have sound advice to offer on how to let the Bible interpret itself, especially regarding passages pertaining to the prophecies of old, as well as of his day, but she also pointed out with unusual insight how one might deal with his own personal relationship with God.

How was this possible? John wondered. Here was this little widow, in her 80s, living in a modest farmhouse way out in a remote area of northern California, who was not only abreast of the times but even ahead of her times in everything that came from her pen. It didn't take John long to learn that Adventists regarded her as a modern-day prophet. Her admonitions were evaluated as being next to the Bible itself in importance.

John scratched his head dubiously when he first came upon this puzzling bit of information. However, the more he read her writings and about her personally, the more certain he became that here was an unusual woman whom God was not only using to help direct honest-hearted Christians like himself to a closer, more meaningful relationship with Him but also showing people their responsibility and relationship to one another and to the world around them.

Especially helpful to him were nine volumes entitled *Testimonies to the Church*, which he found gave him inestimably valuable guidance as he began his work as a young evangelist.

He had not yet been ordained, when in his reading he came upon these startling words: "I cannot understand why our people have so little burden to take up the work that the Lord has for years been keeping before me, the work of giving the message of present truth in the Southern States. Few have felt that upon them rested the responsibility of taking hold of this work. Our people have failed to enter new territory and to work the cities in the South. Over and over again the Lord has presented the needs of this field, without any special results."—*Testimonies*, vol. 8, p. 34.

Another passage stirred John with its challenge to evangelism: "While city missions must be established where colporteurs, Bible workers, and practical medical missionaries may be trained to reach certain classes, we must also have, in our cities, *consecrated evangelists through whom a message is to be borne so decidedly as to startle the hearers.*"—*Ibid.*, vol. 9, p. 137. (Italics supplied.)

Here was a direct commission to him from Ellen G. White, John felt. Yet heretofore he had been directed by the brethren to concentrate on campaigns in Illinois. Sister White had been given this message in 1901. Why hadn't the leaders heeded her directive? He began to pray that the Lord would lead him in answering this straight message demanding action.

The answer that came in short order opened the way for John to do what he felt was the Lord's bidding—get to work in the South. The first door of opportunity that opened was a surprising invitation from P. G. Stanley, president of the Cumberland Conference, requesting him to serve as an evangelist in eastern Tennessee. He and Etta responded promptly to the call.

Until then John had not been a fully accredited worker. But on that climactic day, August 15, 1912, at a camp meeting at Sweetwater, Tennessee, John was ordained to the gospel ministry.

One indication after another came that John and Etta were being greatly blessed in trying to follow the counsel to concentrate on work in the South. Then, in December, 1912, Elder W. H. Heckman, president of the Florida Conference, invited them to begin evangelistic work in Florida. There, in a little more than a year, he and Etta, under the blessing of God, led out in raising up three churches and in building three sanctuaries in St. Cloud, Bowling Green, and New Smyrna.

During his years in Florida John learned more and more effective methods of dealing with the public, keeping in mind that special directive in *Testimonies* that evangelists were to "startle the hearers."

An example of how he worked to obtain favorable attention may be seen in an incident that took place when he was concluding his tent crusade in New Smyrna, Florida. John had just stirred the town with the subject of Saturday versus Sunday observance when a pastor of another denomination placed an advertisement in the newspaper alongside John's ad, announcing that on the following night he would prove Christ changed the Sabbath from Saturday to Sunday.

John took full advantage of the added publicity. He held up the ad and announced that he would not hold a meeting the following Sunday. Instead, he invited his audience to go hear the other pastor, then come back to the tent the following Monday night to review the arguments presented.

The pastor's church was packed on Sunday night, with John sitting near the front, where he and a stenographer recorded the sermon. And the Adventist tent was also overflowing on Monday night when John compared what the pastor had stated with what the Bible says on the subject. The other minister, fearing he might be embarrassed, did not come into the tent but parked his car just outside where he could make his escape if necessary. The audience knew he was there, and laughed aloud when, halfway through the overwhelming scriptural evidence John presented that proved the correctness of the Seventh-day Sabbath, the man noisily cranked up his car and drove off.

In John's tent that night was also the pastor of a rival church of the deflated pastor's. He came up to John after the services, smiling broadly and extending his hand.

"You sure knocked Pastor——— into a cocked hat tonight. Congratulations!" John replied, "All I did was simply turn the Bible spotlight on what he had preached," thinking that he had convinced this man of the seventh-day Sabbath. However, he was surprised to find an advertisement the next day announcing that this preacher would, the next Sunday night, prove that Sunday, the Lord's day, was the Christian's true Sabbath.

A new Adventist convert, Cecil Roper, a stenographer with the Florida East Coast Railway, volunteered to attend and record the sermon for John.

The following Monday night Evangelist Shuler reviewed this sermon and showed how it contradicted the Bible. Now it was the turn of this pastor to leave the tent.

Interestingly enough, however, that preacher couldn't run away from what he had heard. Although he tried to ignore it for the next twenty-five years, it haunted him until he finally sought peace by being baptized as a member of the Seventh-day Adventist church in St. Louis, Missouri.

* * * * *

One successful crusade after another was undeniable proof that John was reaching the people where others had failed. The 27-year-old evangelist wasn't cocky; he had simply discovered a different method of attracting people to the meetings he held. It was not even one particular approach he settled on, either. He seldom, if ever, presented a subject in exactly the same way twice. He tried to maintain a freshness from one campaign to another.

There was one city he knew of that had proved to be practically gospel-resistant to the Adventists. It was Columbia, the capital of South Carolina. At the time, it had a population of 50,000; yet after two experienced ministers had held two campaigns without winning a single convert, and a bit later another zealous worker had been able to win only three or four converts, there were still not enough members to organize a church.

"Dear Lord," John began praying, "if You can use me to open up the work in South Carolina—especially in Columbia—please make it possible."

A short time later John received a telegram that made it

crystal-clear that he was serving a prayer-answering God who was placing His seal of approval on John's earnest endeavors. The telegram, dated August 2, 1914, read, "You have been elected president of the South Carolina Conference. Wire your acceptance. Come to Greenwood, South Carolina, immediately. Your help needed camp meeting services." It was from Elder O. Montgomery, president of the Southeastern Union Conference.

Etta shared John's joy over the appointment, and they began packing. Here was John, three years short of his thirtieth birthday, a conference president! There had never been a conference president that young—doubtless there have been none since. He was president of the South Carolina Conference until 1917, when he was called to the presidency of the Cumberland Conference.

The brethren shared his zeal to begin an effort at once in Columbia, and he began looking for a lot as near as possible to the downtown section. The only one available was a comparatively small space crowded between two buildings on Main Street. There was no room to park, and it was an undesirable location for a number of reasons. But there was no better place, so he rented it and began making plans to hold meetings.

Meanwhile, John had spotted a large open area directly across the street from the State capitol. Although it was being used as a children's playground and had swings and other exercise equipment on it, John couldn't get out of his mind what an ideal location it would be for a tent effort. If only the Lord could intervene someway and make it available instead of the postage-stamp plot they were being forced to make plans for. Then John passed the park on the streetcar one afternoon and was electrified to see workmen taking away the playground equipment.

He discovered that a local real-estate firm had just sold the park to the U.S. Government as the site of a future post office building. John asked the firm to wire the official they had dealt with and inquire whether there would be any objections to the lot being used temporarily for open-air religious meetings. Then he and Etta went into immediate action. They rounded up everyone they knew who had an interest in promoting the tent effort in Columbia, and called for a prayer meeting. It wasn't time for their midweek service, but they held one anyway, in the Shulers' apartment. Each prayer was a fervent appeal for divine intervention at the governmental level. Undoubtedly, they reasoned, it would take time for plans for a new building to be drawn up to fit the location, which would give them the time they needed for the campaign.

Within a matter of a few hours John got a phone call from the real-estate broker telling him that a telegram had been received from Washington. It stated simply: "Government has no objection." They could use the property free of cost for three months.

Joyfully the little group of believers erected the tent, put up their billboards, passed out handbills—and the crowds came. Had John then used the plan he later perfected in Houston, Texas, there would undoubtedly have been a greater success than the effort enjoyed. Nevertheless, John baptized enough converts to begin a new church that was soon to grow to hundreds.

Knoxville, Tennessee, was the next city that challenged John's evangelistic talents. The war with Germany was at its height, so John decided that the prophecy of Daniel 2 would be a fitting opener for his campaign. He took out a newspaper advertisement and distributed handbills displaying in bold capitals the words "Kaiser's Dream Shattered by Bible Prophecy!"

Knoxville's response on the opening night astounded John and his co-workers. The meeting had been advertised to begin at 7:30 P.M., but by seven o'clock every seat in the tent had been taken, and streetcars stopping at the corner were emptying their entire load of passengers, who were then heading for the tent. By opening time there were more people standing outside than there were seated inside. Because of no public-address system, many had to be turned away. It was not until later campaigns that John decided to hold two services rather than disappoint so many.

As it turned out, a number of persistent listeners managed to get there first each night to get seats and hear the entire series. As a result, there were eighty baptisms. John was doing all *he* could to bring Adventism to the Southern cities as Ellen White had envisioned.

15

INTRIGUE

Charlotte, North Carolina, was one fairly large city in the South where a number of traveling evangelists of various faiths had held efforts without singular success. Among them had been several Adventist preachers.

When John heard what a hard nut to crack Charlotte was, he asked the conference for the opportunity to see what he could do there to attract believers and eventually establish a church. Granted permission, he spent some time scouting the city, looking for a suitable site for his tent that would also be in a location to which the general population could walk or come by streetcar.

The most suitable lot he found available was only a block or two from the center of downtown Charlotte, and just off the main streetcar line that ran through the city. The lot was easily accessible to people from the suburbs, who were predominantly cotton-mill employees, as well as white-collar workers and those living in the better section of town. Because of John's choice of this particular lot, a most interesting circumstance developed involving a prominent city family.

The story that was to involve John so dramatically began with a small boy, Vincent Vespain III. Vincent was the only son of a prominent automobile manufacturer, Vincent Vespain, Jr., who, with his father, Vincent Vespain, Sr., had cornered a large area of the financial market by the introduction of a racy, ahead-of-its-time roadster they had named the Wizard.*

Undoubtedly, the car would have been a winner had the stock corporation backing its manufacture been handled wisely. However, personnel in the corporation responsible for its funds were indicted and charged with mismanagement of the company's stock holdings. Consequently, operation of the huge Wizard assembly plant just outside Charlotte ground to a halt, immediately putting the Vespain family in financial difficulty.

The Vespains had always lived well, and beyond their means. The entire family lived together in a large leased Colonial mansion that stood in the best part of town on a slight rise of well-sculptured lawn and hedges and was surrounded by a beautiful flower garden that was the talk of the town.

Members of the family were chauffeured to their business and pleasure appointments in three new cars: a black Packard 12-cylinder touring, an emerald-green King V-8 sport tourer, and a golden brown Apperson 8 Jack Rabbit sports car. Even young Vincent III, at 8 years of age, had his own custom-built roadster that was the envy of every kid in town. Of course it was only a pedal car, but it was long, low, sleek, and had real leather upholstery, headlights, and impressive chrome-plated hand brake, horn, and a crank with a ratchet that fired the imagination of every boy who begged Vincent to let him crank it.

Vincent and his pedal car were confined by parental authority to the sidewalks within six blocks or so of the mansion. He was a happy-go-lucky youngster, but was not so happy as he might have been because his socialite mother insisted on his wearing his hair in the popular Buster Brown bob and keeping him spick-and-span in suits that were more appropriate for some Little Lord Fauntleroy than the real boy he would rather have been.

Poor little Vincent was further burdened by the determination of his mother to have her son have a religious education. She enrolled him in a Catholic school, and took him to his grandmother's Presbyterian church for Sunday school. One or two evenings a week, he went with her to her own favorite Christian Science lectures. In later years Vincent admitted that the only bright spot for him during this time was recess at the Catholic school when he delighted in playing ball with the priests and seeing their robes flying as they ran around the bases.

After school one afternoon, Vincent was tooling along in his resplendent roadster a few blocks from home when he spotted a big tent that had gone up on a vacant lot overnight. He brought his shiny car to a stop beside a young man who was painting a sign outside the tent. His attention had been caught by the outline of several strange beasts the sign painter had begun to work on. One of the beasts had ten heads and ten horns and resembled some kind of dragon; another was something like a leopard with several pairs of wings.

Despite Vincent's obvious interest, the painter simply ignored him. Now, Vincent was not used to being ignored. He beeped his horn to get the man's attention and asked whether the animals were to be on display in the tent. The young man hardly gave him a glance, but went on with his painting in vivid poster colors. When Vincent became more insistent, the artist didn't say Yes. But he didn't say No, either. He simply implied that the only way Vincent was going to find out was to come the following night and bring his parents. He wasn't sure they would let him in unless he was accompanied by his parents.

Maybe the animals were too dangerous, Vincent thought excitedly.

That night at dinner when the whole family was together, Vincent did a bang-up job of whetting everyone's appetite about the strange tent and animals that had come to Charlotte. Would they go? Grandmother said she had promised to take his three girl cousins to a Pearl White matinee the following afternoon. Didn't he want to go? Sure, he never wanted to miss one of the adventure series, but couldn't they go to the tent afterward? Why couldn't they eat downtown after the movie and then go see the animal show?

The suggestion seemed to suit everyone except grandfather, who would have to foot the bill for the show and the meal. But he promised to pick up grandmother, with the four children, and Vincent's mother when he and Vincent, Jr., left their offices downtown. They would have dinner at the club; then they could all go to this freak show Vincent III was so insistent on their attending.

The song service had begun when the big black Packard drove up in front of the tent, and the liveried black chauffeur opened the doors, and the family emerged. The procession of plumed and velvet finery of the women and girls, and the handsomely suited boy and the two elegantly dressed gentlemen, all but stopped the song service as the party headed up the aisle and took seats near the front. Actually, the song leader lost his voice for a moment and found himself beating time soundlessly—accompanied only by Etta Shuler at the piano.

Evangelist Shuler held everyone's attention that night except Vincent III and his cousins, who promptly lost interest when they found the animals pictured were simply some nonexistent creatures someone had dreamed about long ago. Vincent slithered beneath the folding chairs and amused himself by making pairs of green scissors from the stalks of wild onion that sprouted from under the curly pine-scented shavings covering the ground under the tent.

The Vespain family beat a hasty retreat at the close of the meeting, grandmother holding her head high as though seeing through an invisible lorgnette. She had not seen one respectable family from the right side of the tracks in the tent. That settled for her any further attendance. And both the Vespain men were too involved in their rapidly failing business to spend time at the Shuler meetings. But Vincent's mother, Linette, whose failing was following any current religious craze, was hooked. She never missed a night from then on to the close of the campaign. Poor Vincent! He, of course, had to accompany his mother each night. At least he found the meetings to be a great improvement over the dry-as-cinders Christian Science readings he had been forced to attend until his mother dropped them.

The Shuler evangelistic team predicted that this pretty little butterfly of a woman, Mrs. Vespain, Jr., who fluttered in each night in all her jewelry, wearing a new hat for every meeting, would never become a convert. How could such a vain socialite ever become a Christian? But, wonder of wonders, she not only took her stand to become a member of the Seventh-day Adventist faith, but when a call was made for sizable offerings to help build a new church for the hundred or so new converts, Mrs. Vespain dramatically removed all of her rings, bracelets, and necklace (promising to bring more from home) and donated them all to the building program soon to be started.

It was not until later that she learned of the Vespains' financial difficulties. Grandmother's cook had quit because there was actually too little food brought to the kitchen for her to prepare for the family's meals. Still she had been expected to provide three- or four-course meals with all the usual pomp and ceremony. She had long been in the habit of being able to take home all the leavings from the family meals, but of late there had been no leavings to take. She put her complaints into one clipped sentence as she got her things together to leave. "Mizz Vespain," she declared, taking off the French apron the family asked her to wear when she served the table, "there's just too much shiftin' of the dishes for the fewness of the vittles!"

Linette had failed to consult with her husband about her sudden burst of generosity. When she casually told him what she had done, he all but literally went through the roof, saying not only that he had long suspected she had gone out of her mind over religion but that this scoundrel Shuler was nothing but a thief who preyed on the public—especially nitwitted women like his wife. Then, without telling Linette, he took a revolver from his desk and vowed he'd get Shuler the next night.

Had Linette seen the gun, she undoubtedly would have warned John of his danger. However, she merely chalked up her husband's anger to his business difficulties, thinking his wrath would blow over.

At the conclusion of the Shuler tent effort, an upstairs hall had been rented for a meeting place. It was here that Mr. Vespain came to confront the evangelist after the meeting the following night. He stood in the hall outside the door waiting patiently for Elder Shuler to come out. The place had nearly emptied before he came up to the door where Elder J. E. All stood shaking hands with the departing men and women.

"Where's Shuler?" he demanded grimly, keeping his right hand holding the pistol deep in his overcoat pocket.

"Why, he had to go to Raleigh today to see about holding a new series of meetings. Is there something I can help you with?" Elder All asked, recognizing by the man's ashen face that someone was in real trouble.

It is questionable whether Vespain would actually have killed or even wounded Shuler had he been there. Normally he was not a violent man, but under the pressure of his pending bankruptcy, and what appeared to him to justify violence, if necessary, to recover his wife's valuable jewelry, he might have made nationwide news by killing the now-well-known evangelist.

As it turned out, as soon as John returned the following day from what must have been his providentially arranged trip to Raleigh, and learned from Mrs. Vespain of her husband's anger over what she had done, the jewelry was returned. It was not until later, when her husband had recovered from his ire over the incident, that she carefully re-donated a number of her diamonds and other pieces of jewelry that she felt her husband would never miss. However, she kept her wedding and diamond engagement rings she had so spontaneously contributed to the church without her husband's consent.

Not only did she remain an active church member and later on was a devoted, unpaid Bible worker who brought many members into the church, but after ten years of prayer and setting an example for her husband in her Christian life, he too finally became a member of the Seventh-day Adventist Church. Young Vincent III entered an Adventist church school, and four years later was baptized by Elder Shuler at the age of 12. He too has remained a faithful member of the church to this day.

* The family names used here are pseudonyms.

16

HOSTILITY

John Lewis was not one to waste much time reading newspapers, but that afternoon he sat relaxing in the living room of the small apartment he and Etta had rented during the evangelistic campaign being held in Des Moines, Iowa. He had picked up a Sunday paper at a corner newsstand to see whether his two-column announcement about his series of lectures had the dates for the meetings right.

Etta was preparing a light meal in the kitchen. The Shulers had acquired the habit of eating two good meals a day, breakfast at 8:00 A.M. and dinner at about 2:00 P.M., then a light snack about five-thirty. The bread slices she had put into the oven to toast slightly and serve with some freshly sliced peaches and cream turned out darker than John liked. She had picked up a knife to scrape off the carboned corners when she heard a crash of papers and John calling from his high-backed rocker. She ran to him, wide-eyed at his excitement.

"Etta! Look at this!" he exploded, "I've got a hunch they're trying to tell me something." He held up a full-page spread that had come out in the Sunday *Register*. There in bold capitals, the headline shouted: "WHY YOU SHOULD NOT BE A SEVENTH-DAY ADVENTIST." Beneath it were the names of sixty Des Moines ministers who had banded together to discourage their church members from attending the meetings John had just begun.

There was a general statement seeking to belittle "this small offshoot sect" and inviting residents of Des Moines to attend the church of their choice. Then there was a list of the Protestant and Catholic churches within and without the city limits. Each church would be holding a meeting that night on the subject of the Sabbath.

"John," Etta grinned, "it looks like you've got them scared!"

"Maybe *I* should be," John said soberly. "I've never come up against this much opposition all at once in one place. I'm sure I can handle debates man to man, but sixty against one? There's no doubt about it; they've certainly got me outnumbered! It'll be interesting to see how many turn out to our meeting tonight."

"Now, John, dear," Etta said quietly, "remember David and Goliath. Don't let them belittle us. We know we've got God on our side. Just pick up a few of your well-rounded texts, put them in your slingshot, and fire them into your audience. They'll take them back to their pastors, and there'll be nothing but confusion in their ranks!"

Etta was right. And the Shulers were surprised to find almost as many in the tent that night as there had been the night the meetings began. Perhaps some had stayed away to go to their own churches to hear what their pastors had to say.

As John looked down at the hundreds of upturned faces waiting expectantly to hear his answer to the condemnation of their sixty local pastors, he prayed for divine aid in answering the question seen on each face.

He began by asking a question: "How many of you want to be happy?" Without waiting for a show of hands or murmur of assent, he continued, "Of course, each one of you does. There is an innate desire in every one of us that seeks happiness. God made man to be happy. And man's pursuit of cults, isms, philosophies, and religions is an expression of man's quest for happiness. Even Communism is the expression of some peoples' idea of how to be happy.

"Amid all this confusion, uncertainty, disappointment, and delusion of this world, there is One who points the way to true happiness: that is Jesus. He tells us plainly in His Word, 'I am the way.' In His farewell talk to His disciples before He left this world He answered His disciple Thomas's question, 'Lord, . . . how can we know the way?'

"Jesus replied that He was going to prepare a place for them and that He was 'the way, the truth, and the life.' Think what this means to you! Obey Him and you will get to heaven. Take His teachings and you have the real truth. There are not several different ways to heaven. There are not two hundred and fifty ways to heaven, as there are two hundred and fifty Protestant denominations. Jesus is the way.

"He taught that the Scriptures are our only guide for what men should believe. He taught obedience to all the Ten Commandments as one of the necessary conditions for entering heaven."

John pointed out how most Christian religions held in high repute the keeping of the commandments, yet put their own interpretation on the fourth commandment, claiming that Sunday was the Sabbath, when there was absolutely no scriptural foundation for this doctrine.

"If Jesus kept the seventh-day Sabbath when He was on earth 1900 years ago, going to the synagogue 'as his custom was,' isn't He still our example? Has Jesus changed?" he asked. "Has the day He kept been changed? No. The Romans who ruled Palestine in Christ's time called the seventh day the day of Saturn, or Saturday. That was the day Jesus kept, and we have the same weekly cycle they had in Jesus' time. Can't you see that attending worship on Saturday is a part of the way of Jesus?"

John's audience sat in rapt attention as he concluded his answer to the sixty preachers of Des Moines by posing this question, "If you knew there was one church that followed all the essentials taught by the Master 1900 years ago, as outlined in the Scriptures and left us by the Master as our guide for the salvation of mankind, and that Jesus Himself would be a member of that group, wouldn't you unite with them? This is not a difficult question to answer. I think your answer would be Yes.

"If you continue coming each night during these meetings, we will show you clearly from the Scriptures that if Jesus Christ lived in this city today, He would take His stand with this people, who teach and practice His way of life. As for me, the answer to our question settles which is the only church to which I can ever belong."

For the rest of the campaign there was practically standing room only, while John gave overwhelming evidence why his audience should become Adventists. The series closed with one hundred and thirty new members added to the Adventist faith in Des Moines.

It was about this time that some of the conference leaders in the South suggested appointing union evangelists. These would be ministers who had exceptional preaching ability, who could attract the public night after night with their messages. These men would not be assigned duty as regular church pastors, but would be expected to conduct several campaigns a year in the union in which they were working.

John Shuler served as a union evangelist in the Southeastern Union Conference from August, 1918, to August, 1921, and again from January, 1931, to August, 1934. He also labored in the Southern Union Conference from March, 1937, to June, 1939. During these years John concentrated on improving his presentations and devising new methods of attracting audiences. This was ideal preparation for the even more important work that was soon to be pressed upon him—training hundreds of young ministers to conduct evangelistic efforts.

Despite the fact that hundreds were being brought into the church by Shuler as effort after effort was held—evidence that he was being blessed by God in his endeavors—his delivery fell short of perfection. This was painfully pointed out one night after a sermon when he was talking to a group of interested listeners who had remained to ask specific questions. One middle-age woman bluntly inquired, "Mr. Shuler, why don't you take that chewing tobacco out of your mouth while you're talking so we can understand you better?"

John blushed but grinned amiably.

"Well, I don't use chewing tobacco; never have in my life. Unfortunately, you've hit a habit I'm striving to overcome. Even back when I was a boy at home my mother used to tell me I talked like I had a mouth full of mush. Thank you for reminding me I haven't entirely overcome my failing, but I'll keep working on it."

Another failure in his methods became apparent when, after one of his campaigns had been completed and a hundred had been baptized, his Bible workers found it difficult keeping in contact with new members while a church was being organized.

The wife of one of John's assistants, Mrs. J. E. All, tried repeatedly to call on one of the new converts on Sabbath afternoons but never found her in. Finally, cornering her after one of the church services, which were being held in a hall, she asked the young woman why she could never find her at home and asked whether she could call on her that afternoon. She was dismayed to learn that she wouldn't be there that afternoon either, because she and her son never missed the Saturday-afternoon matinee in their neighborhood theater, which featured Harold Lloyd comedies. Obviously proper Sabbath observance and the subject of suitable entertainment hadn't been made clear.

Another new member was distressed to learn from one of her children attending Sabbath school that Adventists had unusual health doctrines. She had prepared a big oyster stew for Sunday dinner when her youngster informed her mother, "Mom, my Sabbath school teacher told us that we shouldn't eat oysters, because the Bible says they're unclean!"

Here again, Elder Shuler was to learn that he and his co-workers were not properly covering all the bases of belief. He immediately took steps to prepare sheets of instructions for all new believers before they were baptized, outlining the essential doctrines held by Adventists as taught by the Bible, giving texts for further study, and directions for contacting Bible workers to discuss any belief that was not perfectly clear.

Later he developed the after-meeting plan to help those who had responded to altar calls, devising a special instruction class that began after the sixth meeting of each crusade.

17

REASSURANCE

Ellen G. White, the little lady out in California who had so inspired John Lewis to evangelize the neglected cities of the South, died in 1915 when the young evangelist had barely gotten started with his campaigns. It was to be one of his greatest regrets that he was never privileged to meet and talk with her. How happy she would have been had she known that under the guidance of the Holy Spirit thousands in the South would be brought into the fledgling church through John's efforts.

Just how many converts John has been responsible for will never be known. But some of the outstandingly successful crusades he remembers include Lakeland, Florida, the home of Etta's parents when she and John were married. John conducted a crusade there in 1932, and ninety were baptized.

That same year John returned to Raleigh, North Carolina, where he had held meetings in 1918. He located an auditorium two blocks from the State capitol for eight dollars a night, and signed a contract for fifty nights. It took the last five hundred dollars in the conference treasury to finance the crusade, at a time when every minister in the conference was receiving only a portion of his salary. But as a result of the meetings a church of one hundred was organized, and as offerings and tithe began to flow into the treasurer's office, the ministers began receiving their allotted wages—even their back pay.

In Greensboro, North Carolina, in 1937, John set up a tabernacle seating about eight hundred people. There were only about ten Adventists in the city at the time, yet on opening night not only was every seat filled but hundreds were standing, both inside the building and crowding into the two big double exits. John apologized for having to ask those standing to leave in order to meet the fire ordinance of the city. "We are sorry to have to ask those who are standing to leave," he announced. "But we promise you that if you will come back next Sunday night we will have two sessions and everyone will have a seat."

And so it was. Each Sunday night for the next ten weeks the tabernacle was packed for double sessions. During the eighth week of the series, Shuler spoke on the "Woman in Scarlet," Babylon, the godless church of the world, and declared the Lord was calling, "Come out of her, my people." He had made no altar call, but the audience, moved by John's appeal to their reason, took his declaration as an invitation to join the church, and 125 got to their feet and went forward to signify their decision to do so.

In 1948, John began holding Sabbath-afternoon meetings in the Grand Avenue church in Oakland, California, after he had conducted a series of lectures in a local theater. On the fifth Sabbath afternoon he preached on the seventh-day Sabbath and concluded by simply asking those in the audience who believed Saturday was the true Sabbath to come forward to the platform to show their intention to keep it. Eighty-six took their stand immediately, and as the meeting continued, another forty joined the others—a total of 126.

A little later, John held a crusade in the Masonic temple in Detroit, Michigan. On the tenth night of the series he boldly spoke out on the mark of the beast, which of course struck home to the hearts of many Masonic Protestants present. He showed how the Catholics were responsible for the change of the Sabbath and, in conclusion, asked for an indication of how many were convinced of the truth he had presented and wished to keep the correct day from then on. Amazingly, without extra urging 250 people crowded to the front. Three of this number later became ordained Adventist ministers.

As a result of John's early experience by which he learned that his lectures were not sufficient to indoctrinate new members satisfactorily, he prepared a series of printed lessons. These lessons were the forerunner of his Bible correspondence course that was soon to become very popular in America and widely used in the world field. However, it was not until 1944, when he was preparing to conduct a series of meetings in a big music hall in Houston, Texas, that he hit upon one of his brightest Bible course ideas to date.

"Etta," he remarked, "if we don't fill those 2,500 seats in the music hall, and have only a crowd of a thousand or less, we're going to look pretty silly. It will weaken our effort from the start. Here's my idea to ensure a good attendance . . ."

John's plan was a simple one. He would place a few large ads in the Houston press five weeks before the effort was to begin, announcing a free Bible correspondence course. All anyone needed to do to enroll was to phone the number given in the ad or send in his name by mail, requesting the lessons.

Etta helped John organize the lessons and file the addresses that came in. She was astonished to list more than 2,000 people who were taking the lessons by the time the campaign opened.

Next, she helped John's team send a letter to all enrollees informing them that the author of the lessons would speak at the music hall on a particular Biblical subject. A handbill was enclosed, and they were invited to write, or phone, for a reserved-seat ticket, which would be mailed them free. The offer was also advertised in the newspapers. The result was that on the Sunday morning previous to the night the lecture series was to begin, more than 2,200 advance reservations had been received.

When the evangelistic team met that morning to pray for the success of the meetings, John remarked, "You don't need to pray for the attendance; we've got it made! Look at this," he went on, holding up a filing box holding the reservations. "But," he continued, "we do need to pray for the Holy Spirit to be with us and to move upon the hearts of those who come out."

That night every seat was filled, and the following Sunday night there was an overflow of 250. The same free-ticket reservation plan was followed in Detroit, Michigan, and in Oakland, California. At these places 4,000 advance reservations were secured, and both series concluded with hundreds being baptized.

The Bible correspondence course was soon spreading as rapidly as a prairie fire. One of the earliest evangelists to adopt the plan was Dallas Youngs, of Williamsport, Pennsylvania, who began using it to back up his radiobroadcasting program. In Los Angeles, California, Radio Evangelist H. M. S. Richards was beginning his Voice of Prophecy broadcast from his office in a chicken coop—which was all that his budget could afford. Operating on such a shoestring, it took much persuasion by Fordyce Detamore, who was using Shuler's correspondence course with his Kansas City broadcasts, backed by Shuler and Youngs before he could be convinced to give it a try. But it proved to be the best decision he ever made. Detamore supplied the lessons, combining his own with Shuler's studies. "I wrote none of them," Richards later admitted, but those lessons became the means of bringing untold thousands into the Adventist Church. Elder Richards gave tribute to the Shuler and Detamore material. He declared, "We've used lots of Brother Shuler's material. He's one of the most prolific and best. His material is among the most solid Adventist writings that we know of. He has been very kind to send us copies of what he does, and his material should be available to all the ministers and evangelists. It is very fine to hand out to new believers and those who are just becoming interested."

The Bible correspondence course has undoubtedly been the means of winning more people to the faith than any other method. Beginning as a tiny "mustard seed," it soon became a great tree with wide-spreading branches. It was later linked with the new plan of home missionary endeavor that became known as the Southern Field School of Evangelism. These were the two mustard seeds of evangelism planted at Greensboro, North Carolina, that became trees whose branches now reach into all the world.

The Southern School of Evangelism revolved around Elder Shuler's conducting two five-month evangelistic campaigns every year in various cities in the South. Each conference sent one of its young ministers to help in these campaigns and to be taught evangelistic methods by Elder Shuler. This plan is today a strong factor in the worldwide evangelism of the Advent Movement.

18

DISTINCTION

Since sunrise John Lewis had spent several hours at his desk in his apartment in Greensboro. It was thirty minutes past his usual breakfast time, but Etta was always hesitant to interrupt him when he was obviously deep in thought. She knew he was hard at work on his brainchild, the Home Bible Course, for which he wished to reduce the main features of the Adventist faith into a series of printed lessons mainly for the use of young ministers who would be following the field school methods. At last he looked up and stared out the window at branches of dogwood, festooned in their newest spring fashion of white blossoms trimmed in fern green, dancing gracefully in the early-morning breeze.

Taking advantage of the momentary break, Etta was about to remind him that breakfast had been ready for some time, when he mused: "Etta, do you realize you're married to an old man of 52 years?"

"Why, John! What a silly thing to say!" She waved a dish of his favorite hot cereal under his nose to catch his attention, then grabbing his hand, led him to the kitchen table. After grace, she began upbraiding him gently.

"You're not an old man in any sense of the word. You're as active physically and mentally as you could possibly be. Even so, it might not hurt to request a six-month leave of absence—is that what you're thinking of?" she suggested hopefully.

"Why, of course not!" he exclaimed, shocked at such a suggestion. "I just wish the good Lord had made me twins, or triplets, or better yet, quadruplets, so I could get more done in my evangelistic program. I'm certain that if Ellen White were alive she would still be pointing out all the unentered cities in the South where we haven't a single believer because no efforts have been held there."

"But John, dear," Etta reminded him, "your idea of the field school is catching on and was officially adopted by the Southern Union Conference last year [1937]. More and more young ministers are learning by observing your methods. What more could you ask?"

Etta's point was well taken, John had to admit. If only more young ministers interested in becoming evangelists could be observers of his program so they could get out on their own more quickly. But there was no way he knew of that would make the conference willing to send a group of men—all at the same time—to study his approach to evangelism, and there were no textbooks on the subject they could study on their own. He and Etta began praying that some way would be developed by which young evangelists could be trained more quickly and in larger numbers, not just one at a time.

The answer to their prayers came unexpectedly a little more than a year later, in 1939, from a source the Shulers had never dreamed of. The General Conference brethren had been watching the number of converts John had been adding to the church in the South over the years—the average being between 130 and 140 at each campaign. If only they had more men with the know-how and down-to-earth practicality who could organize a complete program as well as Shuler could, they reasoned.

Since many promising young ministerial students, fresh out of college, attended the Theological Seminary in Washington, D.C., the brethren at headquarters came up with the idea of initiating an extensive course of training in the technique of successful evangelism at the Seminary. It was obvious that John Shuler was the man for the job, and the invitation was sent. Would John take the position?

Both John and Etta were amazed when the call came. Was not this the direct answer to their prayers? Yet John, ever modest despite his unparalleled successes in evangelism, shook his head at the very thought of accepting.

"Etta, how can I, a high school dropout who has never received an hour's training in any of our denominational schools, become a member of the teaching staff of the Seminary, which is composed of men who hold M.A.s, Ph.D.s, D.D.s, or LL.D.s from colleges and universities all over the world?"

Etta, too, realized that the invitation had its drawbacks, even if her husband was the only man she could think of who was qualified for the job. She agreed with John that his name on the Theological Seminary rosters would look pretty foolish if he were listed truthfully: John L. Shuler, S.H.K.—School of Hard Knocks!

They laughed at the incongruity, and mentally he began composing his letter declining the honor. He would explain how impossible it would be for him, with his obvious lack of education, to stand before a class of highly educated young men and try to teach them anything. He could well imagine their derision at being asked to give their undivided attention to an old duffer such as he. Besides, he would point out, evangelism was his whole life. How could he give up his very lifework—even for such a worthy project?

But the brethren were way ahead of him. Before he had written his letter, he received further confirmation of the offer, outlining their plan in detail. They were asking him to conduct evangelistic crusades for five months each year and teach at the Seminary the remainder of the time. The conference that used Shuler's services would pay his travel expenses, provide an apartment for him during the crusade, and at the close send a check to the Seminary to cover his five months' salary.

"Etta, dear," John grinned ruefully, "it'll never work. I'll never get any calls under those conditions." He was well aware that some years before, the General Conference had set up a similar program for another well-known and capable evangelist. The only requirement was that the local conference using the services of the evangelist assume the expenses of the crusade. But not a single invitation had come in.

"But, John," Etta interposed, "perhaps conditions have changed since then. And this still looks like it may be the answer to our prayers. Why not give it a try for a year? That is, if your pride will let you be humiliated by all those—those young pharisees!"

"Oh, let's not call them that!" John laughed. "If the young seminarians are all well trained in the Scriptures as they're supposed to be, they'll know the Lord hates a proud look. Maybe they'll learn to put up with me!"

And so it was that the Shulers accepted the call and moved to Takoma Park. The modern, newly erected Theological Seminary building was next door to the General Conference headquarters, which adjoined the Review and Herald Publishing Association. Beside it was the fine Review cafeteria where John and Etta enjoyed having many of their lunches together, and meeting many people connected with the General Conference and the Review.

Right from the start it was seen that Etta had been right in her suggestion that times might have changed since the other evangelist had been at the General Conference and had received no calls from any conference. One difference was that many conference presidents were personal friends of John and had firsthand knowledge of what he had accomplished in his Southern crusades. They were eager to extend their invitations the moment his availability became known. There was never any lack of calls for John's crusades during the thirteen years that he carried on his teaching program at the Seminary.

During those years he developed three courses in evangelism, "Evangelistic Methods," "Pastoral Evangelism," and "Securing Decisions," which carried graduate credit at the Seminary. In addition, John responded to numerous calls to present studies on evangelism at ministerial institutes and workers' meetings. He even taught his courses in a Seminary Extension School at Newbold College, near London, England, and spent thirteen months "down under," dividing his time between ministerial institutes held in Australia, New Zealand, and the Fiji Islands.

John's fear of being looked down upon by his fellow professors at the Theological Seminary and the students in his classes proved groundless. As a self-taught theologian, he could hold his own with the best of them. His vast knowledge of the Bible and his self-taught grasp of history (he had even learned Latin) put him on a practical par with many an LL.D., D.D., or Ph.D. But when it came to presenting his course in evangelism, and he opened his huge scrapbooks of clippings that he and Etta had gathered through the years of many of his campaigns, the entire faculty and student body was mightily impressed.

John's new assignment was of inestimable personal value because in order to teach others he had to know the subject thoroughly himself. In obtaining that knowledge he had to work for it, think about it, and most of all, pray about it. He was inspired by the wisdom of Solomon, who declared that "a wise man is strong; yea, a man of knowledge increaseth strength" (Prov. 24:5).

That strength came through in John's personality and was transmitted to the young men who were sitting in his classes. Those of them who were students of Sir Francis Bacon may have recalled one of his well-known quotations appropriate for the sessions: "Men have entered into a desire of learning and knowledge . . . seldom sincerely to give a true account of their gift of reason, to the benefit and use of men: as if there were sought in knowledge a couch whereupon to rest a searching and restless spirit; or a terrace for a wandering and variable mind to walk up and down with a fair prospect; or a tower of state for a proud mind to raise itself upon; or a fort or commanding ground for strife and contention; or a shop for profit or sale; and not a rich storehouse for the glory of the Creator and the relief of man's estate."

John's students soaked up his knowledge as though they were learning the secret of levitation or how to walk on water. Among those young men were some who would later become prominent leaders in the Advent Movement: Neal Wilson, W. A. Fagal, George Vandeman, Kenneth Wood, D. R. Guild, Roger Holley, A. E. Cook, W. T. Clark, Fordyce Detamore, and Orley Berg, to name but a few.

An unsolicited testimony was received years later by Elder Shuler from W. A. Fagal, director of the Faith for Today TV series. He wrote: "I never see your name or hear about you without feeling gratitude in my heart for all that you did for me back in the early days of my ministry. My experience at the Seminary was most rewarding. I went there specifically to study with you so as to be able to do a better job in evangelism. You did not disappoint me in any way. I will always feel a great deal of love and appreciation in my heart for you, and what you have meant to me through the years. May God bless and guide you always in your service for Him."

In a letter to Elder Shuler, John W. Osborn, at the time Ministerial secretary of the Pacific Union, wrote, "If I were to name the one evangelist in the denomination whom I feel to have made the greatest contribution toward training other evangelists, I would have to say that it is John L. Shuler."*

---

* It is impossible to know with any certainty how many ministers received instructions from Elder Shuler in his Seminary classes, extension schools, ministerial institutes, and so on. Perhaps a conservative estimate would be 3,000.

19

ISLANDERS

From November, 1949, to January, 1951, the Shulers served in the Southern Hemisphere.

Etta and John were thrilled to travel by steamship to their appointment "down under." It was nothing like the tiny coastal vessel they had taken long ago during that ill-fated trip from Baltimore to Jacksonville, but was a giant passenger ship provisioned with all the luxuries available for vacationers. This experience Etta described as "heavenly!" The weather was ideal, and they enjoyed every moment of the week-long voyage from San Francisco to Australia. From there they flew to Suva, capital of the Fiji Islands, where John was scheduled to hold a crusade.

Suva, considered one of the garden spots of the Pacific, had an ideal climate, the thermometer never rising above 90° F. and never sinking below 63° F. And there was no malaria for the white man to worry about. It was a spot as near to paradise as one could wish for, with lovely hibiscus glowing like orange flames against the dark-green foliage, and other flowers of every color of the rainbow growing in profusion everywhere.

"Oh, John!" Etta sighed blissfully, all but speechless at the beauty of Suva as their taxi took them from the airport through wide streets lined with gracefully swaying coconut palms, to their downtown hotel. And this was to be their home for the next four months while John conducted an evangelistic campaign in the city! Etta was ecstatic.

But John, lost in thought, did not comment. He was already considering the problem of how he would present his message to these people. He knew that the kinky-haired blacks thronging the streets were in reality not too many years removed from cannibalism, although they were now generally considered Christianized under British rule. He sat in the front seat of the taxi and let Etta sit in the back with the white Adventist mission woman who had met them at the airport and was conducting them to their temporary quarters.

The woman introduced John to the driver, whom she happened to know. He was named Mauki, she told them, and was the son of a chief, but had been kidnapped to be a copra laborer and taken away from home when a youth. Mauki said nothing but grinned widely with two rows of the most beautiful teeth John had ever seen.

Mauki was perhaps about 30 years old. It was hard for John to tell, not yet being used to judging the people's ages. At first they all seemed to look exactly like carbon copies of one another. The illustration was particularly apt, John was thinking, because the man was peculiarly black. He was not blue-black or purple-black; he was plum-black. John judged him to weigh about 110 pounds, but he was well proportioned and of a muscular build. He seemed to John to typify the average Fijian.

"You Christian, Mauki?" John asked, wondering both how the man would reply to the question factually and whether he would use the pidgin English he had been told was commonly used in the islands. But Mauki's reply told him nothing about the language. He answered simply, "Yes, master!" in a soft, mellow voice that had a mystic quality.

Was Mauki's aura somehow linked with his colorful past? John wondered.

The meetings, held at the city hall, were well advertised and well attended. John was aided by Australian workers who had been sent in to help him; he, in turn, was to aid them with his new Stateside approach.

It was a new experience for John, seeing that sea of black faces before him.

Elder Shuler spoke slowly and thoughtfully to his audience—weighing his words as he strove to reach the Fijian mind. They seemed to be getting his message without its being translated into pidgin English, as he at first thought might be necessary. What John did not know was that the Lord had arranged, by means of that Suva crusade, to spread His message to other remote islands in the South Pacific. Attending the meetings were young natives, chosen by the government for their superior intelligence, who had been sent to Suva to receive medical training. They had come from Guam, Samoa, the Ellice Islands, and other islands in the South Pacific where there were limited facilities and workers to provide adequate health care for the islanders. Night after night the auditorium was packed, and when the series closed and further Bible classes were held for those who had taken their stand, every one of those young medical men was in the group getting last-minute indoctrination. John had no idea what was taking place at the time. All he knew was that this group of assorted fuzzy-wuzzies gave evidence that they were memorizing, word for word, practically everything he said to them.

John and Etta met their appointments in Australia and New Zealand, where they collaborated with Dr. Charles Wenigar, who had been sent by the Seminary to conduct courses in speech during John's institutes. Among those attending the special three-week sessions held near Sydney were two hundred ministers from all sections of Australia. A similar three-week ministerial institute was held near Aukland, with seventy ministers attending from the North and South islands of New Zealand.

From New Zealand, the Shulers returned to Australia, where John conducted a four-month campaign in a suburb of Sydney and held a field school for a group of ministers.

While they were in Australia, John began to notice that Etta was obviously not well. Outwardly she appeared normal, with good color, but she began to slow down in her reactions, and her replies to his questions were sometimes mere monosyllables. Then one day he and Etta went downtown to do some last-minute shopping before returning to the United States, and John lost her in the crowd. Some thirty minutes later he found her standing on a street corner with a blank expression on her face. When he took her by the elbow and asked her where she had been, she couldn't tell him. Her mind was a complete blank—she didn't know where she was or who she was.

John hailed a taxi and took her back to their hotel, where within a few minutes she seemed to recover. But her mind was blank regarding what had happened to her downtown. Had she had a slight stroke? John wondered. But there was no time for a physical checkup, because they were to fly back to the States almost immediately, and Etta had seemingly recovered sufficiently to make the trip.

However, it was this experience that was to provide John with his answer to General Conference president W. H. Branson's invitation to conduct a crusade and field school in South Africa. Frightened by what had happened to Etta, he turned down the call and decided it was time to retire from the Seminary as well as from his strenuous evangelistic campaigning. Although he did file for retirement, John still had too much fire for God in his system, so he was never to know what it meant to be fully retired. He continued conducting short crusades, took part in institutes and workers' meetings, and began working on an unbelievably endless list of books. At this writing, at 95 years of age, he is still at it.

After John left the Fiji Islands, the young men who had been baptized finished their medical training and went back to their respective island homes. None of them were contacted for a number of years. Then F. A. Crofoot, secretary-treasurer of the Far Eastern Island Mission, took a business trip from the Palau Islands to Guam, during which his ship called at a number of villages in the Marshall and Caroline islands. The ship stayed a few hours at each of the islands, and Brother Crofoot went ashore to ask whether there were any Seventh-day Adventists living there.

He learned that the director of public health for the island of Majuro, a Dr. Hickings, kept Saturday. Brother Crofoot contacted him and found he was one of the men who had been baptized as a J. L. Shuler convert. Dr. Hickings had never met an Adventist since, and was, of course, delighted to meet Brother Crofoot, who arranged to have Sabbath school quarterlies sent to him.

On the island of Ponape in the Caroline group, Crofoot found Dr. Jano, a medical doctor, and Dr. Paul, a dentist. Both men had been converted by Evangelist Shuler's meetings but had had no further contact with the Adventist Church. However, they did have a number of friends with whom they had been studying the Bible.

Pastor Crofoot's experience was repeated at the island of Truk, where he found that the radio operator for the Trust Territories Administration was also one of the men sent to Suva for training and had become a convert under Elder Shuler. He had a group of between twenty and twenty-five friends meeting regularly with him for Bible studies. He was also conducting a small Sabbath School, but had no denominational supplies to work with.

The ship stopped at other islands, until Brother Crofoot had found eight places where there were other lone Shuler contacts. These scattered believers were subsequently organized into what became the Mission Church Group and were supplied with Sabbath school quarterlies and other helpful literature. Not long afterward, government authorities permitted them to be visited regularly, and future contacts were made for the entry of other workers.

Of course, John and Etta were delighted to learn the outcome of their Fijian adventure.

20

REMARRIAGE

John Shuler's "retirement" became effective on November 1, 1952. He fully intended to try to take it a little easier after that, but it didn't work out. It never would, he was to learn.

In an attempt to get off on the right foot for retirement, he sold his home in Takoma Park and moved to southern California, where he and Etta found a lot in a quiet, rural beauty spot named Yucaipa. Here, on a gentle slope near the base of picturesque mountains that were snowcapped most of the year, he built a modest little home where he expected to concentrate on writing some of the many books he had in mind.

The site was chosen not only for its beauty but also because it was conveniently near the Loma Linda Medical Center, where he or Etta could receive any kind of medical attention that might be needed.

Etta's health had been going downhill ever since she had had her strange loss of memory in Australia. Her increasing muscular weakness, which remained undiagnosed, soon kept her from doing most of her housework, and it became a constant chore to find suitable help in their home. Consequently, John decided it would be easier to get the help Etta needed if they lived right in Loma Linda. So they sold their Yucaipa garden spot and made the move they thought would help solve their problem.

Although the Shulers felt more at ease in their new home, nestled among the year-round fragrance of orange orchards and practically next door to the hospital, their difficulty remained unsolved. It was still next to impossible to find and keep competent household help. After one disturbing incident after another, John suggested selling out and going to live at an Adventist retirement center at Paradise Valley.

Etta loved her own home and resisted moving out as long as she could. However, she agreed at last that the work of keeping the place up was too much for them. So again they sold their house and made the move to Paradise Valley.

The two years they spent together in Paradise Valley were not the happiest of their lives, but they made the best of it. Etta, with her happy, outgoing nature, soon made many friends. But they missed living in their own home where they could revel in their independence.

Their quarters at the manor were anything but pretentious. Yet John and Etta were not demanding; they were simply used to something a bit better than what they now had. And they had trouble with the food. Many of the folk there were on salt-free diets, so the rest of the residents had to be content with dishes that were, more often than not, flat and tasteless.

About two years after they moved, Etta lapsed into a coma from which she never recovered. Within two days she died. John's companion and constant co-worker for sixty-one years was laid to rest at Redlands, where some years before he had purchased space in a mausoleum for both of them.

Sadness at the loss of his lifelong loved one caused John to retreat into a shell of introspection that was to last for a number of years. He tried to bury himself in his writing, but memories of his youth and the high points of his career kept crowding in upon him one after another.

This quiet time in John's life gave him opportunity to reflect upon how miraculously God had led him from the day he left the coalpits to enter the pulpit. He saw that nothing is trivial in the progression of a man's life—that every occurrence had played its part in conditioning him for his life's eventual purpose.

He could now smile at the trials of those early years and the strict economy required. How well he remembered saving the cost of a pullman fare by sitting up all night on the train. Many a time he had made a meal of canned milk and cinnamon rolls while traveling, and had paid as little as twenty-five cents a night for a room during his campaigns. He was thankful that those days of such strict economy were past. He could now relax with the comfortable retirement income granted him by the General Conference and devote himself to his writing.

John found comfort in memorizing large portions of the Bible. In addition, he widened his horizon by studying the writings of many other religious writers and philosophers. One particular quotation brought a thin ray of light into this dark corner of his experience: "There is no better armor against the shafts of death than to be busied in God's service."

Perhaps John should give the widows at the manor credit for at least starting him thinking about the possibility of remarrying. Whatever the reason, he did begin wondering what it would be like to marry a second time. He and Etta had been such perfect partners that it was difficult to imagine finding a replacement. Should he marry a second time, might it not be concluded that his first wife had failed him? Still, by taking a second wife, would he not be paying his first wife the highest compliment by indicating that she had made him so happy that he wished to be so a second time?

Whatever the logic that won him over to accepting the idea, of one thing John was certain, the second Mrs. John Shuler did not live at the Paradise Valley Manor—as heavenly as the name might sound. Only one woman came to mind. She was very attractive, extremely well-groomed, and—though he was not monetarily motivated—was well-fixed financially. Best of all, she was eligible.

He had known Bernice Chaney for years—ever since he was president of the Florida Conference. She had attended Shuler's efforts at Lakeland, Florida, in 1932. He knew she had taken his Bible study course, and remembered she had read a number of his booklets. Their paths had crossed years later in Loma Linda. She had now been a widow for thirteen years and was living as a companion to the widow of Elder Glenn Calkins in the Calkins home in Loma Linda.

Bernice and Etta had often chatted over the Calkins' fence when Etta took her daily walk. They had become good friends since they both had lived in Florida and had much to talk about. Once John had phoned Bernice and asked her whether she wanted to come to a meeting he was having in Yucaipa where he would be showing some of his color slides. He thought it would be a good diversion for Alice Calkins, at least. He didn't think Bernice would be much interested since she was a well-traveled person, but the two ladies had come and they had had opportunity to trade pleasantries after the meeting.

John learned that Bernice had left Florida after her husband's death and had lived in Escondido in a mobile home. There she had been contacted and asked to live with Mrs. Calkins after Elder Calkins died. Alice Calkins very much needed a companion, so a conference official contacted Bernice and pleaded with her to come up for a month at least and do what she could for Alice until a permanent replacement could be found.

Bernice, conscience-stricken, living as she was in luxury, prayed about it and decided that this was little enough missionary work to do. She consented to stay no longer than six weeks and ended up remaining nine and a half years. Eventually, she convinced the Calkins estate administrator she should be released from caring for the big Calkins house, which was much too large for just two women. She proposed buying a smaller home of her own in Yucaipa, where she would continue to care for Alice. It was agreed, and the two women moved to Yucaipa. While there, the Shulers went to Paradise Valley, and Bernice lost track of them.

However, when she read an announcement in the *Recorder* of Etta's death, she sent a card of condolence to John, but he did not reply. It was later, when John learned from the *Recorder* that Alice Calkins had died, that he wrote Bernice a letter of condolence and asked whether he could come up to see her "about a personal matter." Bernice was suspicious at once. She couldn't think of anything personal he would have to talk about unless it was marriage, and after being a widow all these years she didn't think she wanted to give up her freedom.

Bernice had one son, a physician with offices in Escondido. When she phoned him and told of receiving Shuler's provocative letter and that she wasn't minded to answer, Dr. Chaney replied: "Say, if you've got a chance of marrying Elder Shuler, jump at it! You're a foolish woman if you don't. I took a Bible Doctrines class under him when I attended Washington Missionary College, and that man's a brain. You couldn't go wrong marrying him!"

Intrigued by her son's prodding, Bernice dropped John a note saying it would be all right for him to come up. It turned out to be just a friendly visit, and she reciprocated by going down to see what Paradise Valley was like. She took a room there for a few days so they could further compare their likes and dislikes. One of their shared hates was bubble gum. Their fervor had a compelling origin.

John had appeared at Bernice's door in Yucaipa with consternation written all over his face. He had just gotten off the bus down at the highway and had walked up to her place with his overnight bag in hand.

"Bernice," John began, "I'm so embarrassed! I was sitting near a youngster on the bus and when he got off I went over to sit where he had been, not noticing he had left a huge wad of bubble gum on the seat. When it was time to get off I walked down the aisle trailing strings of gum. Look at me! I'm a mess!"

"Well, come on in. We'll see what we can do about it. I've got some spot remover. Let's see whether that won't take it off." She returned in a moment.

"Bend over!" she commanded. He did, and she did—bending her efforts to remove the big sticky glob. All of it came off after continued applications of the solvent.

Perhaps it was the bubble gum that helped draw them together, for it wasn't long afterward that they set their marriage for sometime in September; the exact date was uncertain. Bernice's first wedding anniversary was September 17, and John's was September 18, and they didn't like the idea of setting another wedding too close to either of those dates.

Doctor Chaney was elated at their decision, offered his services as best man for John, and suggested that the ceremony take place in his home. Bernice's youngest granddaughter could stand up with her for the big event. But before a date could be set, John got a call to go to the Soquel camp meeting to give a series of studies on the work of the Holy Spirit. That was the first of August.

Bernice, having much to attend to, decided not to go with him. The first thing she had to do was buy a new dress that would be suitable for the wedding. This done, she began packing her suitcase for whenever they decided to tie the knot. John left on a Friday.

Sabbath morning Bernice got a call from her son.

"What are you doing?" he wanted to know, surprised she

hadn't gone to church in Yucaipa.

"Oh, I've got so many things to think about, I'm just taking it easy today. I'm sitting here listening on the radio to the sermon from the Hill church in Loma Linda. Why?"

"I just got to thinking that you should have gone with Elder Shuler. You love camp meetings. Why don't you fly up and join him? You'll enjoy it," he suggested.

"Well, I guess I could; but where would I stay? At this late date I probably wouldn't be able to find a place to lay my head," Bernice countered.

"Phone John. He'll find a place for you," her son replied.

Like some flighty teen-ager, Bernice placed a call to the camp meeting switchboard, asking that Elder Shuler be paged.

"I don't need to; he just walked in the door!" the operator replied.

When Bernice told John she might come up if he could find her a place to stay, she was shocked at his reply: "Come on up. There's no problem. Let's get married here on Thursday!"

Following a flurry of excitement, getting blood tests, a wedding license, and a place to stay, John and Bernice were married in Elder Amundson's office at five o'clock that Thursday, August 8, 1974. Bernice's bouquet was a spray of artificial flowers snatched from one of the campground altar vases. And in her haste to pack *everything*, she forgot her wedding dress. It was hanging in the back of her closet in Yucaipa. So she was married instead in the suit she had made the trip up in. Elder Amundson's secretary witnessed the ceremony.

The new Mrs. Shuler, describing their life together, says: "We've had such a wonderful, *wonderful* life together! For the first three years we didn't stay home at all. Right away John got a call to Hawaii, where he was asked to hold a ten-day meeting. We stayed there for a month, enjoying the islands. When we returned to Paradise Valley, we were back only days—just long enough to wash our clothes and repack our bags—then we were off to Gladstone, Oregon, where John took all the early-morning camp meeting services. It rained every day we were there!

"I expected John to be in misery while there because when we were in the islands he had slipped and fallen, cracking one of his ribs. He could hardly get out of bed the first morning of the camp meeting, but the moment he stood behind the pulpit and prayed for God's blessing on the meetings, his pain left him and never returned!''

As for John, the marriage turned out to be not merely between two people—it was a union between two kindred spirits. The bond helped perfect the natures of both of them, each balancing the deficiencies of the other, yet combining their strength of character to ennoble each other. There were two rocks upon which their souls were anchored: the one was God, and the other—for John—was a good wife. For Bernice it was a good husband.

21

EXCELSIOR!

For years John had dreamed of writing evangelistic books for people who might study their way into the Advent message. He had been able to put out some of that type of material during spare time squeezed between his crusades. After Etta died, and before he remarried, he decided he would concentrate on writing. This would relieve his loneliness and at the same time allow him to focus on themes he felt demanded his keenest thinking. He is still writing.

One of John's aims was to discourage long, drawn-out, emotional altar calls commonly used by evangelists. He felt that the decisions people made during these calls were motivated more by emotion than by reason. To be solid and lasting, John was convinced they needed to be based on the certainty and surety of Jesus and the Adventist faith.

John determined to teach aspiring young evangelists by precept and example that long appeals were entirely unnecessary if sermons were thoughtfully and prayerfully prepared and so appealed more to a listener's reason and call to duty to God than to his emotions.

To help both the potential reading convert and the evangelist, many booklets and pamphlets were published that came from John's pen. Among them (some written before, but most after, his retirement) were *Christ, the Divine One, The Coming Conflict, Is the End Near? The Coming Man of Destiny, The Great Judgment Day, Helps to Bible Study, Public Evangelism, Give Your Guilt Away, When God Intervenes, By Water and By Fire*, and *God's Everlasting Sign*.

Between times, John began holding a few short crusades, speaking to groups at workers' meetings and at prayer meetings, and showing some of the more than 7,000 color slides taken during his travels.

Then came a union conference session, held in Jacksonville, Florida, in 1970, to which John was invited to present six lectures on "Securing Decisions." While there, he was honored by the Southern Union Conference for his contribution to the advancement of the ministerial work by his establishing "The Shuler Lectureship in Methodology in Evangelism." John particularly enjoyed his return to Florida and renewing his acquaintanceships in Jacksonsville, where he had pastored the only church in his long ministry outside of his lay ministry at Farmington.

There were other diversions. A pleasant surprise invitation came to address a group of ministers on what he considered the most important principles of successful evangelism. In presenting the series he revealed that he was not above applying the rules of successful salesmanship used in the workaday world. At the conclusion of the session, the Voice of Prophecy presented him with a plaque expressing appreciation for his forty-one years of active evangelistic ministry, begun when he was a lad of 18.

One of his biggest surprises came when he received an invitation to return to St. Cloud, Florida, as guest of honor at the dedication of a new church building named the John L. Shuler Memorial church. John had organized a little church of twenty-eight members there in 1913 sixty-four years before. The building had long since been outgrown, and a new one had just been built.

John was surprised to find that the only living charter member was Etta's nephew, Kenneth Rothrock, who spoke at the dedication. Kenneth had been present as a 10-year-old boy at John and Aunt Etta's dandelion wedding in 1910, in Flora, Illinois. He moved to Florida later to live with his parents in St. Cloud.

Looking back, John could trace how the tabernacle type of evangelism slowly lost its effectiveness. Public interest had started to wane during the 1920s, despite the fact that there had been many successful campaigns since then. However, conditions had continued to grow more adverse, and it had taken a great deal of effort to start the ball rolling before each campaign. But once John had caught the interest of the public, the crowds had continued coming.

John felt that this decline in interest was but another sign of the times. The spirit of evangelism, he believed, was waning in

Adventist churches throughout America, as well as in Western Europe and the British Isles. Nevertheless, there was no loss of zeal for the work of the Master in John Lewis. His indomitable spirit was undimmed and undiminished.

Actually, John's fervor was greater in his closing days of public evangelism than it was at the height of his successes. With other workers, advancing years narrowed their field of operation, but not John's. He determined that no rocking chair would ever capture him. There was one important way he could capitalize upon his past: through the years stenographers had transcribed his sermons verbatim, typed them up, and mimeographed them, and John had made them available to young ministers who were welcome to revamp or use them as they wished for their own campaigns. In later years John used Soundscriber machines that helped capture his messages "hot off the gridle," as one man described them.

This material had served its purpose then; now it provided a valuable source for other material he began to work on. One of the most important of these was a manuscript he entitled *The Search for Truth*. The book was edited so as to be different in its approach from any Adventist book previously published. In it John stressed the prophecy of Revelation 14 as being fulfilled in the mission of Seventh-day Adventists, as Isaiah 40:3 was fulfilled by the mission of John the Baptist and Isaiah 61:1, 2 by the mission of Jesus to this earth.

The 139-page book was intended to lead the reader to unite with the Advent Movement. There was no emotional appeal. One reason after another was secured together to construct a dependable scaffold so an honest seeker for truth could erect his own spiritual tabernacle for the worship and service of God, in harmony with Bible instruction.

Although past his ninetieth birthday at that time, John wrote in longhand far into the night and often rose at four o'clock in the morning to work on his manuscript. Before *The Search for Truth* was submitted to the publishers, he let a church member read it. This brother was so impressed with its potential effectiveness as a soul winner that he sent the Review and Herald Publishing Association a check for $10,000 to be used to circulate the book among non-Adventists.

Before the book was off the press, the Voice of Prophecy ordered 3,000 copies, and Faith for Today, 2,000 copies, to be mailed free to non-Adventist graduates of their Bible correspondence courses.

H. M. S. Richards, Sr., speaker emeritus of the Voice of Prophecy, commenting on the then 90-year-old evangelist's dedicated dissertations, wrote to a friend: "J. L. Shuler is one of the world's wonders, still producing this good material. As the Scripture says: 'They shall still bring forth fruit in old age,' and 'He shall be like a tree planted by the rivers of water, that bringeth forth his fruit in his season' (Ps. 92:14; 1:3)."

John's Heaven-given incentive was to have great purpose and greater achievement. It is doubtful that any member of the Adventist Church—or perhaps of any other denomination—can equal Elder Shuler's record of writing six books in his ninetieth and ninety-first years, with all of them approved for publication.

John had no thought of breaking any records in his record-breaking endeavor. He was spurred by an overpowering desire to serve God to the best of his ability; then came his love of his fellow man so that he sought to use every avenue he could to point them heavenward. And there was, of course, his love of work itself. John had long since learned that there is no truer or more lasting happiness than the knowledge that one is doing, day by day, the best work he can, the work he likes best, and the work that has Heaven's stamp of approval.

In the life of John Lewis Shuler these words have assuredly been fulfilled: "The afternoon sun of his life may be more mellow and productive of fruit than the morning sun. It may continue to increase in size and brightness until it drops behind the western hills."—*Selected Messages*, book 2, p. 221.

22

AN INTERVIEW WITH JOHN L. SHULER

Q Elder Shuler, were you born in Farmington, where your story begins?

A. No. I was born March 2, 1887, in the little town of Angus, Iowa, near Des Moines, and was taken by my parents to Farmington when I was still quite young.

Q. Were you able to go back to visit your parents and try to convert them?

A. Neither of my parents were religiously inclined, although they were both good moral people. Knowing what I do now, I believe that I could have overcome that barrier if it had been done tactfully. My sister Oce did become interested in the Advent message and took Bible studies from a minister in Canton, Illinois, and had decided to become a member of the church. She was making arrangements to come to California to have me baptize her, but died of cancer before she could make the trip. My father died at age 47 of lung and heart disease shortly after I left home for the last time, and I was never able to reach him spiritually.

Q. After the loss of your only child, did you and Etta ever consider adopting?

A. No. Etta and I were so dedicated to the life we had to live, in which we moved constantly from one campaign to another, that we felt we could not do justice to rearing a family, especially on our limited income.

Q. Did you ever meet Ellen White?

A. No. I have always regretted never having met and talked with Mrs. White, but she died in 1915, shortly after I began my ministry, and I never had the opportunity of seeing her.

Q. Billy Sunday died in 1935. Did your paths ever cross?

A. No. I did visit Billy Sunday's home in Winona Lake,

Indiana, years after his death, where I met his widow. She was a most gracious lady and spent some time showing me his many scrapbooks of clippings collected over the years.

Q. Are you a self-inspired author, or does the publishing house or Ministerial Association assign you topics on specific subjects?

A. My books are entirely my own production. Years ago the *Signs of the Times* and *Review and Herald* used to ask me to write on particular subjects, but now I write upon the subjects I choose.

Q. Aside from seeking the leading of the Holy Spirit, which is, of course, most important, what advice would you give ministers in their endeavors to reach souls?

A. Study how the mind works, how it formulates a decision. Know how to prepare your sermons so as to incorporate your listener's basic needs artfully and arouse his desire to love and serve God. Help people to want to obey God because they have learned to love Him.

Q. What would you name as the crowning achievement of your life?

A. I have to give a three-part answer to that, but each part is related to my aid to ministers. First, my thirteen years spent as a teacher in the Seventh-day Adventist Seminary, where I was able to coach hundreds of young ministers on how to reach hearts through proved evangelistic methods. Second, the special methods that brought success to my crusades. Third, the helps I have made available to ministers—both with prepared sermons I have supplied them, and through the booklets I have written that they might give new believers, helping them to understand the meaning of salvation, the victorious life, and righteousness by faith.